Template — A pattern that is made from a durable material, such as poster board, manila folders, or clear plastic sheets. A template is placed on the fabric; then, a marking tool is used to draw around the template directly on the fabric. We recommend clear plastic sheets for making templates for piecing. They remain accurate through multiple uses and enable you to see the design of fabric through the template. Using clear plastic templates is especially helpful when you are working with a directional fabric and must line up the grain line with the design of fabric.

QUILTING SUPPLIES

There are many things to consider when purchasing your quilting supplies. If you are a beginning quilter, you may not wish to invest a large amount of money in supplies, but consider buying quality products. Your tools could last a lifetime and the quilt will be easier to make and last years longer.

Appliqué needle — These needles, sometimes called "sharps," are thinner than other sewing needles. Used for appliqué, basting, and hand piecing. A size 10 or 12 sharp works well.

Batting — The middle layer of a quilt. Batting is most commonly available in polyester, cotton, or a blend of polyester and cotton. We recommend that beginners choose a low-loft polyester bonded batting. A low-loft batting is thinner or flatter than a high-loft batting and is easier to quilt through. When batting is bonded, it has a finish or has gone through a process to keep the fibers from separating and coming through the fabric. Amount of batting needed is found under **Selecting Fabrics**, pg. 3.

Clear plastic sheets (optional) — May be used for making templates. Clear plastic sheets are durable, remain accurate after many uses, and can easily be placed on the fabric along straight grain or along design of fabric.

Cutting mat — A special mat designed to be used with a rotary cutter.

Fabrics — Used for quilt top, backing, and binding. Types of fabrics to choose and amounts needed for the quilt are found under **Selecting Fabrics**, pg. 3.

Freezer paper — Used for making cardboard templates and for stabilizing fabric for signing and dating the quilt.

Iron — Used for pressing prewashed fabrics before cutting out quilt pieces and for pressing seam allowances. Steam may be used, but take care not to stretch or distort quilt pieces. Do not slide iron on fabric; pick it up and place it back down.

Light table or sunny window — Used when marking placement lines for appliqué pieces and marking quilting lines on medium or dark fabrics.
To trace designs using a window, tape design to window; tape fabric over design on window and trace design.
If a sunny window is not available to you, you may wish to make a temporary light table. If so, you may purchase an 18-20" piece of heavy glass or Plexiglas™ from a local hardware store. If edges of glass are rough, cover them with duct tape. (**Note:** *Always use caution when working with glass.*) Open the leaves on your kitchen table or place two small tables a small distance from one another. Place a lamp beneath the table and place the glass on top of the table *(Fig. 5)*. Tape design to be traced to the glass; place fabric over design. You will be able to see through the fabric and trace design.

Fig. 5

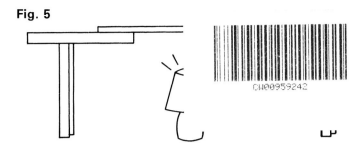

Lightweight cardboard (optional) — May be used for making templates. White poster board or manila folders are good choices.

Marking tools — Used to draw around templates on fabric and to mark placement lines and quilting lines on quilt top. There has been much discussion recently about the different kinds of marking tools available to the quilter.
Fabric marking pens have been used in recent years to mark quilting lines on the quilt top. These marks are easier to see than some pencil marks, and are washed away with water. Since the marking pens have only been available for a relatively short time, we do not yet know their long-term effects on fabric. Still, many quilters use them and are very happy with the results. If you choose a fabric marking pen, be sure to follow the manufacturer's instructions for removing the marks.
Lead pencils, silver colored pencils, and white fabric marking pencils are also very popular with quilters. Keep any pencil sharp to ensure the accuracy of the quilt block, as thick lines will add width to quilt pieces. A mechanical pencil is very helpful in that the lead is always sharp, allowing you to make a thin, clear line. Lead pencils work well on light colored fabric and silver or white pencils work well on dark colored fabric. Press down with pencil only as hard as is needed to make a visible line. Marks need to remain on the fabric until you are through quilting and should be easily removed. Most markings are removed when the fabric is washed. A soft, white fabric eraser or white art eraser can help remove pencil marks. Do not use a colored eraser; the dye may discolor fabric.
To choose marking tools, **test** different markers **on scrap fabric first** until you find the ones that give you the desired results. If marks are not easily removed from fabric, try another marking tool.

Needle threader (optional) — Helps to thread a needle with a very small eye, such as a quilting needle.

Permanent fine point marker — Used to mark clear plastic sheets when making templates and to sign and date quilt. Test marker to make sure it will not bleed on fabric or wash out.

Quilt soap — Mild soap designed to remove dirt, oils, and finishes from fabrics without the use of chemicals that may shorten the life of the quilt. A small amount of mild laundry soap may be substituted, but is not ideal. Do not prewash fabrics without soap, or finishes may be left on fabrics that may shorten quilt life.

Quilting hoop — Designed to securely hold the three layers of a quilt (top, batting, and backing) while you quilt. An embroidery hoop is designed to only hold one layer of fabric and is not considered a substitute for a quilting hoop. We recommend that you quilt with a 14" or 18" hoop. A larger size will make it difficult to reach the center with the hand that is underneath the quilt. Also, quilting with a hoop of this size instead of using a large frame allows you to quilt in your lap, and makes your quilting portable.

Quilting needle — These needles, called "betweens," come in numbered sizes such as 8, 9, 10, and 12. The higher the number, the shorter the needle. Betweens are shorter and thinner than regular sewing needles, allowing you to work through layered fabric easier and to make small stitches. We recommend that beginning quilters use a size 8 or 9 needle. More advanced quilters may wish to use a size 10 or 12 in order to achieve smaller stitches.

Quilting thread — This thread is stronger than regular sewing thread and has a coating that makes it slide easily through the quilt layers. Cotton-covered polyester quilting thread is strong and readily available. At first, you may wish to choose a neutral color so that variations in the size of stitches will not be obvious.

Rotary cutter (optional) — A cutting tool made up of a round, sharp blade mounted on a handle. May be used to cut fabric. A rotary cutter is especially helpful in cutting long strips of fabric, such as sashing and border strips. Should be used with a cutting mat and ruler.

Ruler — Used when marking straight lines on templates and on fabric. A clear plastic ruler with ⅛" measurements marked crosswise and lengthwise aids in accurate markings. An 18" quilter's ruler has such markings and is commonly used. An Omnigrid® ruler, which is thicker and made of harder plastic than a quilter's ruler (but also has ⅛" markings), also works well, especially when using a rotary cutter.

Scissors — A pair of sharp scissors is needed for cutting fabric. A separate pair of scissors for cutting out templates is recommended. Fabric-cutting scissors should not be used for cutting out templates as the blades will soon become dull and make cutting fabric difficult. You may also wish to keep a small pair of scissors handy for clipping threads.

Seam ripper — Used for ripping out stitching that must be removed.

Sequin pins or trim pins — These pins are shorter than regular straight pins and are easier to work around when appliquéing. Available in ½" and ¾" lengths; the ¾" may be easier to handle.

Sewing machine (optional) — May be used for piecing quilt blocks, assembling quilt top, attaching binding, and making pillows. Photo model quilt and pillows were machine pieced.

Sewing thread — Used for basting, piecing, and appliquéing. Cotton or cotton-covered polyester thread is strong and readily available. If you are working with all dark fabrics, use a dark thread. If you are working with all light fabrics, use a light thread. Most often in quilting, you will be working with a variety of colors and shades; in this case, use a neutral color, such as ecru.

Straight pins — Used to secure fabric pieces for sewing. Pins should be sharp and clean so that they will slide easily in and out of the fabric.

Thimble — Used when sewing and quilting to protect the finger that pushes the needle through the fabric. Thimbles are available in metal, plastic, and leather, and in many sizes. Using a thimble may seem awkward at first, but with practice, you will not want to work without one.

Typing paper — Used in the Paper Basting method of appliqué.

¼" wheel (optional) — Sometimes called Quilter's Wheel. May be used to draw the cutting line when preparing to cut out quilt pieces for hand piecing. *(Note: In hand piecing, templates are made for drawing the sewing line rather than the cutting line.)*

SELECTING FABRICS

The following fabric list and instructions are for using six different fabrics to make the quilt, as was done on the photo model. The six fabric categories are a very light background fabric (muslin works well), a light fabric, two medium fabrics and two dark fabrics.

Amounts needed for quilt*:
  3 yds — 44/45"w background fabric
  ⅔ yd — 44/45"w light fabric
  ¾ yd — 44/45"w medium fabric #1
  4 yds — 44/45"w medium fabric #2 for piecing and outer border
  3½ yds — 44/45"w dark fabric #1 for piecing, sashing, and inner border
  1 yd — 44/45"w dark fabric #2
  1½ yds — 44/45"w fabric for binding (We used medium fabric #2.)
  3 yds of 90"w fabric **OR** 6 yds of 44/45"w fabric for backing (We used muslin.)
  90" x 108" piece of low-loft polyester bonded batting
  1½ yds — 44/45"w fabric for temporary borders (optional)

*Add ½ yd if using directional fabrics.

100% cotton fabrics are best for quilting. Choose a good quality, tightly woven fabric that is not see-through. 100% cotton fabrics hold a crease better, fray less, and are easier to quilt through than cotton blends. Check end of fabric bolt for fabric content and width.

The colors you choose for your quilt are very important. Color is seen first, even before design and workmanship. Light colors emphasize an area of a quilt, while dark colors cause an area to recede. The colors you choose should have contrast to make them a little more exciting to the eye. If you are not sure that two fabrics have enough contrast, take a small piece of each to a copy machine and make a black and white copy of them. Above all, when selecting your color scheme, make sure the colors are pleasing to you. If a fabric matches or blends, but is not a fabric you really like, change it. You will be much happier with the quilt in the long run.

A mixture of solids and prints is pleasing to the eye. You may wish to use all solids or all prints. If you choose all prints, be sure to vary the size and type of the prints to add interest and contrast. For example, you may try flowers, dots, and hearts.

If you wish to use a directional fabric, such as a stripe or plaid, consider its position in the quilt and take care when cutting out pieces. Stripes and plaids are the most obvious directional fabrics, but you should also take care when working with a small design printed in rows. Buy an additional ½ yd if using directional fabric. This enables you to line up arrows on templates with the design of the fabric if it is printed off grain, rather than following the straight grain of the fabric. The design of the fabric overrides the grain. Also, sew these pieces carefully, as you may be working with bias edges which stretch easily.

In piecing lessons, diagrams are given for each block, along with a fabric key that identifies which fabrics were used in the photo model quilt. Once you have chosen all the fabrics for your quilt, make your own key by cutting a small piece from each fabric and taping it to a piece of paper. Label each fabric piece with the appropriate fabric color, such as medium fabric #1.

PREPARING FABRICS

All fabrics should be washed, dried, and pressed before you begin work on your quilt. Even if you do not plan to wash your quilt in the future, it is important to wash the fabric before you begin. Washing removes sizing, pre-shrinks fabric, and checks for colorfastness. Washing also makes the fabric easier to quilt through and will remove chemicals that may shorten the life of your quilt.

Dark colors such as red, blue, green, or black may bleed when washed. To check these colors, fill a sink about half full with very warm water. Place one end of fabric in water and agitate with your hands. Gently squeeze water from fabric. If water is not clear, wash fabric separately until rinse water runs clear. If fabric continues to bleed, choose another fabric.

To wash fabrics, separate fabrics by color and machine wash in warm water using a small amount of soap made for quilts and fine fabrics, or a small amount of mild laundry detergent if quilt soap is not available. Do not use fabric softener. Rinse fabric at least three times to make sure all finishes are removed from fabric. Dry fabrics in the dryer, checking long fabric lengths occasionally to make sure that they are not tangling. To make ironing easier, remove fabrics from dryer while they are slightly damp.

MAKING TEMPLATES

Making templates is a very important step in quilt making. If your templates are inaccurate, you will find it impossible to piece quilt blocks together correctly. Use a ruler when drawing straight lines for templates. Place finished template over pattern to check for accuracy.

Patterns for the piecing templates in this book have two lines: a sewing line (dashed line) and a cutting line (solid line). **The cutting line is traced for machine piecing;** a ¼" seam allowance is included. **The sewing line is traced for hand piecing;** you will add the ¼" seam allowance to these pieces when they are cut out. Patterns for appliqué templates have only one line — the sewing line. These patterns do not include a seam allowance; you will add the seam allowance to these pieces when they are cut out.

FROM CLEAR PLASTIC SHEETS
For clear plastic templates, place plastic sheet on pattern. Using a permanent fine point marker, trace dashed line for hand piecing or solid line for machine piecing. Trace arrow for straight grain. Write pattern letter and name(s) of block(s) on template. Carefully cut out template along traced lines.

FROM LIGHTWEIGHT CARDBOARD
For cardboard templates, lay freezer paper shiny side down on pattern. Use #2 pencil or permanent marker to trace dashed line for hand piecing or solid line for machine piecing. Trace arrow for straight grain. Do not cut out pattern at this time. Place freezer paper shiny side down on cardboard. With iron set at cotton setting (with no steam), place iron on freezer paper for 3-5 seconds; do not leave iron on freezer paper longer than 5 seconds or freezer paper may permanently fuse to cardboard. Cut out template and remove freezer paper. Write pattern letter and name(s) of block(s) on template.

CUTTING OUT QUILT PIECES

FOR MACHINE PIECING
Lay template on **wrong** side of fabric, lining up arrow with straight grain. This will help keep the fabric from stretching. (**Note:** *If your fabric has a directional pattern, such as a stripe or plaid, line up arrow on template with design of fabric, even if it is not on straight grain.*)

With marking tool at an angle (to prevent skipping) and with tip against edge of template, carefully draw around template. Since templates contain seam allowances, there is no need to leave a space between quilt pieces. Line up edge of template with line of previously drawn piece and draw around template. The pieces will share a cutting line; **Fig. 6** illustrates fifteen squares being drawn on fabric. Cut out quilt pieces along drawn lines.

Fig. 6

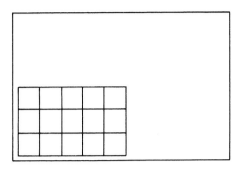

It is important to transfer dots to fabric that are at the corners of some patterns; these will help you sew set-in seams and align pieces that do not match exactly, such as a triangle being sewn to a square.

FOR HAND PIECING
Lay template on **wrong** side of fabric, lining up arrow with straight grain. (**Note:** *If your fabric has a directional pattern, such as a stripe or plaid, line up arrow on template with design of fabric, even if it is not on straight grain.*)

With marking tool at an angle (to prevent skipping) and with tip against edge of template, carefully draw around template. This is your sewing line. Leaving at least ½" between drawn shapes to allow for seam allowances, repeat for required number of quilt pieces (**Fig. 7**). Cut out each quilt piece approximately ¼" outside drawn line. (**Note:** *A ¼" wheel may be used to mark the cutting line. Place tip of marking tool in center of wheel and roll around template to mark cutting line; then, cut out each quilt piece along drawn cutting line.*)

Fig. 7

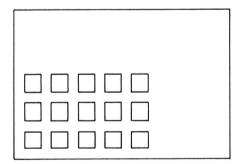

Disregard the dots that are at the corners of some patterns. These dots are for use in machine piecing and are not necessary for hand piecing; this is because hand piecing involves sewing only from one end of a sewing line to the other and not sewing into seam allowances.

SPECIAL SITUATIONS
Some quilt pieces are to be cut out with the template reversed. For reversed pieces, simply turn template over before drawing around template.

Some templates must be placed on fold of fabric. Fold fabric with right sides together. Finger press fold. Place specified edge of template on fold. Draw around template and cut out quilt piece.

PIECING AND PRESSING

Accuracy is very important when piecing. To help you remember the placement of the pieces, lay out pieces as they will appear when the block is completed. Then, following individual instructions for piecing order, pick pieces up as you need them, sew them together, and lay them back down with the other pieces.

When piecing some blocks, ends of seam allowances will extend past edges of pieces; trim ends of seam allowances even with edges of pieces (**Fig. 8**).

Fig. 8

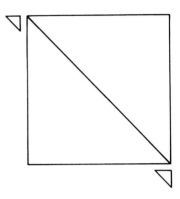

MACHINE PIECING

Set sewing machine for approximately eleven stitches per inch. Use a needle suited for cotton weight fabric, and make sure the needle is sharp. For many sewing machines, the measurement from the needle to the outer edge of the presser foot is ¼". If this is the case with your machine, you may use the presser foot as a guide to sew a ¼" seam allowance. If not, measure ¼" from the needle and mark the seam allowance on the sewing machine with a piece of masking tape. Or, use a ruler and marking tool to mark sewing lines ¼" from raw edges on wrong side of each quilt piece.

Use regular sewing thread (not quilting thread) to piece by machine. Sew on scrap fabric first to check upper thread and bobbin thread tension and make any adjustments necessary to the machine before you begin to piece.

Any time you are using straight pins while piecing, remove the pins as they get close to the sewing machine needle. Do not sew over pins, as it may cause the needle to move or break, or may even jam the machine.

To begin piecing, place pieces right sides together and match raw edges; pin pieces together. For pieces that do not match exactly, such as long triangles in Friendship Star, insert a pin through dot at one corner of each piece; repeat at corner on opposite end of seamline (**Fig. 9**); pin pieces together and remove pins at corners.

Fig. 9

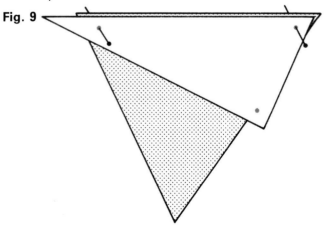

In most cases while machine piecing, you will sew from one edge of the fabric to the other, sewing into the seam allowances (**Fig. 10**). However, when you will be sewing into a corner, such as in the LeMoyne Star, you will only sew between the dots, backstitching at beginning and end of sewing line (**Fig. 11**). This will allow you to pivot the piece in order to sew the next seam precisely. Situations in which it is necessary to sew between the dots are noted in piecing lessons. (**Note:** When sewing from one edge of fabric to the other, it is not necessary to backstitch at beginning and end of stitching. Stitches will be secured by intersecting seams.)

Fig. 10

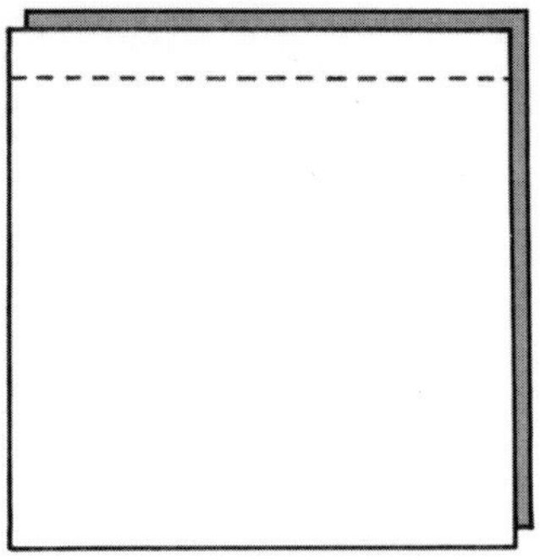

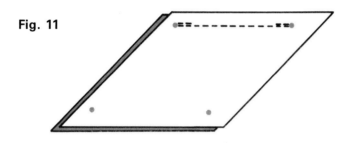

Fig. 11

HAND PIECING

To begin piecing, thread a sewing needle with a single length of sewing thread; make a small knot in one end. Place pieces right sides together and carefully match drawn lines. Insert a pin through one end of drawn line on both pieces; repeat at opposite end of drawn line (**Fig. 12**). Pin pieces together and remove pins at corners.

Fig. 12

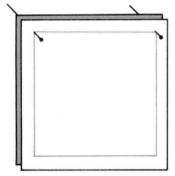

Take a backstitch at one end of drawn line. Using a Running Stitch (approximately 7-10 stitches per inch), stitch pieces together along drawn line, checking both sides of fabric as you sew to make sure that your stitches are straight, even, and directly on drawn line. With practice, your stitches will also be small. Do not sew into or across seam allowance; backstitch at end of drawn line *(Fig. 13)*. Knot and clip thread.

Fig. 13

PRESSING

Planning your pressing is very important. The following guidelines will help you decide which way, and when, to press seam allowances. In machine piecing, press seam allowances as you sew. In hand piecing, press when you complete a section or a block rather than pressing each seam as you sew. In hand or machine piecing, seam allowances are almost always pressed to one side, not open; this gives strength to the seam. The seam allowances are generally pressed toward the darker fabric. However, to reduce bulk in certain areas, it may be necessary to press the seam allowances toward the lighter fabric or even press them open.

When you are matching seams to sew rows together, seam allowances must face opposite directions. Also, seam allowances from strips such as in Rail Fence and Grandma's Fan should be pressed in one direction to distribute bulk. Pieces that radiate out from the center such as LeMoyne Star should also be pressed in one direction, either clockwise or counterclockwise.

To help distribute bulk after sewing through seam intersections, it is necessary to press seam allowances open at the intersection. In hand piecing, use your finger to open seam allowances at the intersection; press *(Fig. 14)*. In machine piecing, you will need to use a seam ripper to remove stitches in the seam allowance past the intersection; then, press seam allowances open. This does not weaken the seams; they are still secured where the stitching lines cross.

Fig. 14

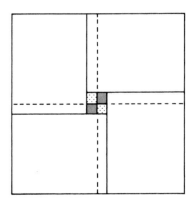

In order to eliminate shadowing, which is a dark fabric seam allowance showing through a light fabric, trim the darker seam allowance slightly narrower than the lighter seam allowance.

MAKING PILLOWS

Any quilt block may be made into a pillow. If desired, you may add a border, a ruffle, lace, or cording to the pillow top before adding the backing.

1. For pillow top, piece desired quilt block according to corresponding lesson, referring to **General Instructions** as necessary.
2. To add a border, cut two 12½" long strips of fabric the desired border width. Matching right sides and raw edges, sew strips to top and bottom of quilt block using a ¼" seam allowance. Cut two strips of fabric the length of the pieced block (including attached border strips) and the desired border width plus ½" for seam allowances. Matching right sides and raw edges, sew strips to sides of quilt block using a ¼" seam allowance.
3. For pillow top backing, cut a piece of fabric and a piece of batting 3" larger on each side than pillow top (including border, if added). Follow **Lesson Twenty-three** to mark quilting lines, to baste pillow top, batting, and pillow top backing together, and to quilt the pillow top. Trim pillow top backing and batting even with pillow top.
4. For pillow backing, cut a square of fabric same size as pillow top.
5. To make a ruffle, cut a strip of fabric twice desired finished width plus ½" for seam allowances and twice outer dimension of pillow top (measure pillow top on all four sides, then double measurement). Ruffle strip may be pieced. Press short ends ½" to wrong side. Fold strip in half lengthwise with wrong sides together and press. Baste ¼" and ⅛" from raw edges. Pull basting threads, drawing up gathers to fit pillow top.
6. To make cording, measure outer dimension of pillow top and add 2". Cut a bias strip of fabric 1½" wide and determined length (strip may be pieced). Lay purchased ¼" cord along center of strip on wrong side of fabric; fold strip over cord. With zipper foot, machine baste along length of strip close to cord.
7. See **Fig. 15** for placement of trims. Start at bottom edge of pillow top and 1" from end of trims. One at a time, baste trims to right side of pillow top with finished edges toward center of pillow top and raw edges facing outward. Clip seam allowances at corners.

Fig. 15

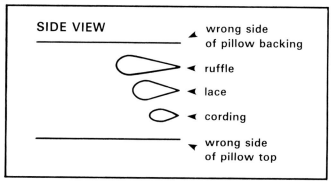

SIDE VIEW — wrong side of pillow backing
ruffle
lace
cording
wrong side of pillow top

8. Opening ends of cording, cut cord to fit exactly. Fold fabric around cord. Insert one end of cording into the other end; turn top end of fabric under ½" and baste in place. With zipper foot, sew cording in place along seamline.
9. Hand stitch ends of ruffle together.
10. With right sides together, sew pillow backing to pillow top, leaving an opening at bottom edge. Turn right side out, carefully pushing corners outward. Stuff with polyester fiberfill or insert pillow form and sew final closure by hand.

Making The Sampler Quilt

Follow Lessons 1-21 to cut sashing and border strips and to piece blocks. Lesson 22 will teach you how to add sashing and borders. Lessons 23-25 will help you mark, quilt, and finish your sampler quilt. Finished size of each block is 12" square. When you complete Lesson 25, you will have a 78½" x 93" quilt, comforter size for a double bed.

Lesson One

In this lesson you will learn how to prepare fabrics for piecing and how to cut border and sashing strips.

Before cutting any fabric, follow **Preparing Fabrics**, pg. 4, to wash, dry, and press all fabrics to be used in the quilt.

To make sure you have enough fabric for the long border and sashing strips, they should be cut first, before cutting out quilt pieces. These strips are cut along the length of the fabric to keep them from stretching and to eliminate the need to piece strips. Take care to cut strips the exact widths given. To be cautious, you may wish to cut the strips longer than needed and trim to required length. Because it is easy to confuse the strips after they are cut, pin a piece of paper on each strip on which you have written the measurements of the strip. Strips may be cut traditionally, using scissors, or they may be cut using a rotary cutter. Read the following sections thoroughly and follow either method to cut strips.

TRADITIONAL METHOD

The traditional method involves measuring and marking with a ruler and marking tool, then cutting with scissors. Use a ruler to mark a straight line along lengthwise grain next to selvage; cut selvage from fabric. Mark and cut 3" wide strips for sashing and inner border as shown in **Fig. 1a**. Mark and cut 9½" wide strips for outer border as shown in **Fig. 1b**.

Fig. 1a

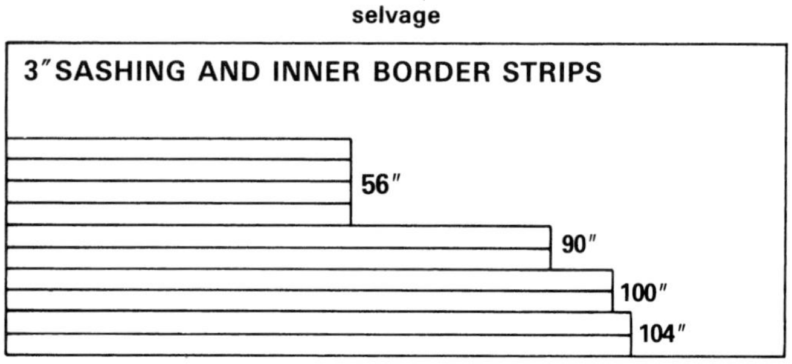

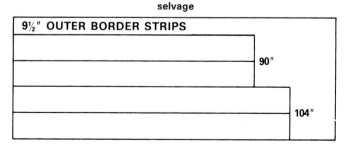

selvage

Fig. 1b

selvage

ROTARY CUTTER METHOD

Using a rotary cutter can make the job of cutting sashing and border strips quick and easy. Along with a rotary cutter, you will need a cutting mat made for the cutter, and a thick see-through ruler with vertical and horizontal markings. A thin ruler may work, but the rotary cutter may skip onto the ruler or nick the edges. *(Note: Always use caution when working with a rotary cutter; keep blade protected when not in use.)*

Place cutting mat on a flat surface. Lay fabric on cutting mat with one raw edge in front of you and one selvage on the left *(Fig. 1c)*. Place ruler on edge of fabric, aligning one of the vertical lines over the selvage. Place the blade of the cutter against the edge of the ruler. Beginning with the cutter near you and rolling the blade **away** from you, roll blade on the mat before you reach the fabric. Keeping the blade against the edge of the ruler, roll the blade away from you while holding ruler down firmly with other hand. Move next section of fabric onto mat and repeat to trim selvage from desired length of fabric.

Fig. 1c

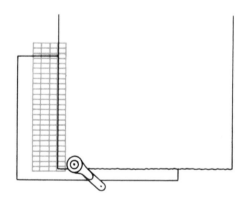

Beginning with trimmed edge of fabric on the left, place ruler on fabric with the measurement for the width of the strip on the trimmed edge of fabric. For example, to cut the 3" wide sashing strips, place the 3" vertical marked line of the ruler on the trimmed edge of fabric and use rotary cutter as described above to cut strip. If your ruler is narrower than the strips you are going to cut, measure and mark width of strip on fabric; then, line up edge of ruler with markings and roll cutter along edge of ruler to cut strips. Cut 3" wide strips for sashing and inner border as shown in **Fig. 1a**. Cut 9½" wide strips for outer border as shown in **Fig. 1b**.

Lesson Two

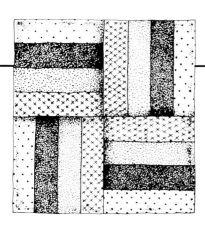

In this lesson you will make the **Rail Fence** block. You will learn to make templates and learn basic piecing skills, including sewing through intersections.

Fabric Key

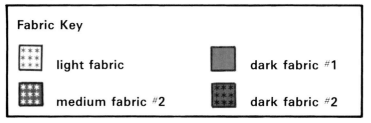

light fabric

dark fabric #1

medium fabric #2

dark fabric #2

1. Follow **Making Templates**, pg. 4, to make template A.
2. Follow **Cutting Out Quilt Pieces**, pg. 4, to cut out the following:
   A — four from light fabric
   A — four from medium fabric #2
   A — four from dark fabric #1
   A — four from dark fabric #2
3. Follow **Piecing and Pressing**, pgs. 5-6, to sew four A's together to make Unit 1 *(Fig. 2a)*. Repeat to make a total of four Unit 1's.

Fig. 2a

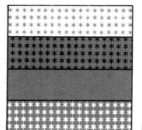

Unit 1

4. Sew two Unit 1's together to make Row 1 *(Fig. 2b)*.

Fig. 2b

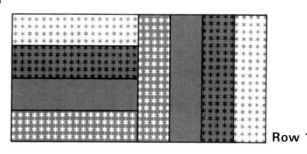

Row 1

5. Sew two Unit 1's together to make Row 2 *(Fig. 2c)*.

Fig. 2c

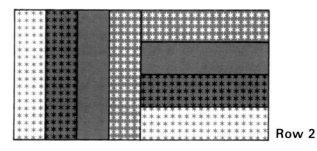

Row 2

6. Follow **Sewing Through Intersections** to sew Rows 1 and 2 together to complete Rail Fence block *(Fig. 2d)*.

Fig. 2d

SEWING THROUGH INTERSECTIONS

To sew through intersections by machine, place pieces right sides together and match seams, making sure seam allowances are facing opposite directions. To prevent fabric from shifting, pin seam allowances down. Sew across intersection *(Fig. 2e)*.

Fig. 2e

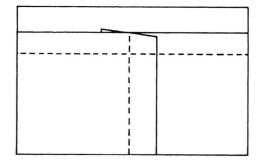

To sew through intersections by hand, place pieces right sides together, match seams, and pin. Sew pieces together along drawn line until you reach the intersection. Take a backstitch and insert needle through intersection *(Fig. 2f)*. Backstitch on other side of intersection and continue to sew as before.

Fig. 2f

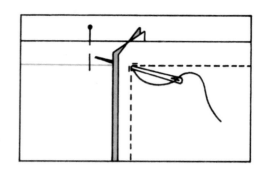

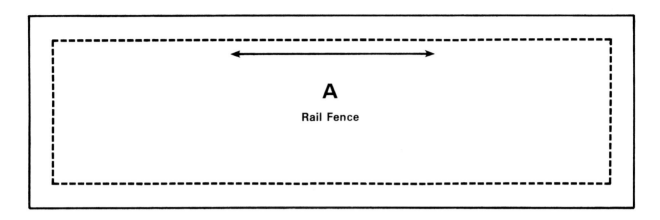

A
Rail Fence

Lesson Three

In this lesson you will make the **Double Nine Patch** block and practice sewing through intersections.

Fig. 2f

Fabric Key

▦	background fabric	▦	medium fabric #1
▦	light fabric	▦	medium fabric #2

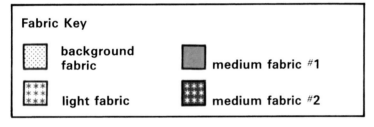

1. Make templates B and C. *(**Note:** Template C is one of several templates in this book that will be used for more than one block. Copy all block names onto your template for future reference.)*
2. Cut out the following:
   - B — five from light fabric
   - B — twenty from medium fabric #1
   - B — twenty from medium fabric #2
   - C — four from background fabric
3. Sew one medium fabric #2 B between two medium fabric #1 B's to make Unit 1 *(Fig. 3a)*. Repeat to make a total of ten Unit 1's.

Fig. 3a

Unit 1

4. Sew one light fabric B between two medium fabric #2 B's to make Unit 2 *(Fig. 3b)*. Repeat to make a total of five Unit 2's.

Fig. 3b

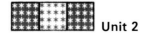

Unit 2

5. Sew one Unit 2 between two Unit 1's to make Unit 3 *(Fig. 3c)*. Repeat to make a total of five Unit 3's.

Fig. 3c

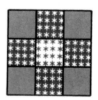

Unit 3

6. Sew one C between two Unit 3's to make Row 1 *(Fig. 3d)*. Sew one Unit 3 between two C's to make Row 2. Sew one C between two Unit 3's to make Row 3.

Fig. 3d

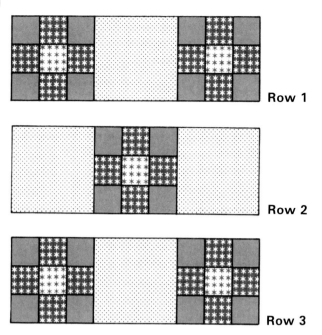

Row 1

Row 2

Row 3

7. Sew Rows 1, 2, and 3 together to complete Double Nine Patch block *(Fig. 3e)*.

Fig. 3e

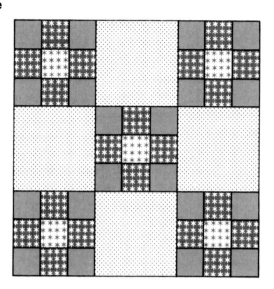

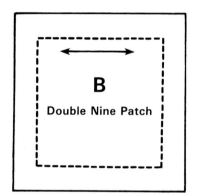

B
Double Nine Patch

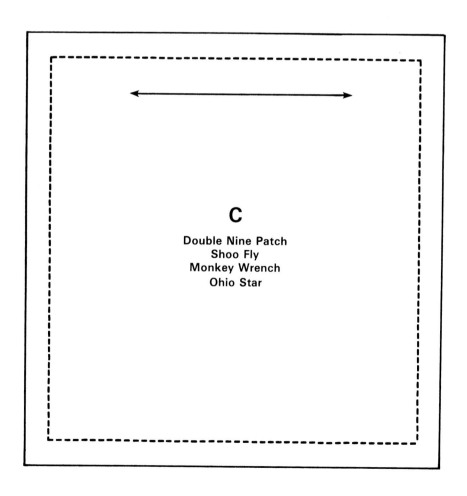

C
Double Nine Patch
Shoo Fly
Monkey Wrench
Ohio Star

Lesson Four

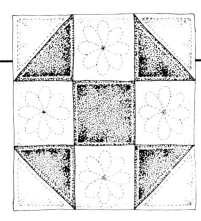

In this lesson you will make the **Shoo Fly** block and learn about sewing triangles with bias edges together.

Fabric Key

 background fabric

medium fabric #1

---

1. Make template D. You will also need template C (previously made).
2. Cut out the following:
   C — four from background fabric
   C — one from medium fabric #1
   D — four from background fabric
   D — four from medium fabric #1
3. Follow **Sewing Triangles With Bias Edges Together** to sew one background fabric D to one medium fabric #1 D to make one Unit 1 *(Fig. 4a)*. Repeat to make a total of four Unit 1's.

Fig. 4a

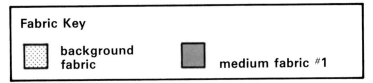 Unit 1

SEWING TRIANGLES WITH BIAS EDGES TOGETHER

Because bias stretches, be careful not to stretch fabric when sewing pieces with bias edges together. After sewing the seam, carefully press seam allowances to one side, again making sure you do not stretch the fabric. These precautions will help all pieces in the block fit together precisely.

4. Sew one background fabric C between two Unit 1's to make Row 1 *(Fig. 4b)*. Sew medium fabric #1 C between two background fabric C's to make Row 2. Sew one background fabric C between two Unit 1's to make Row 3.

Fig. 4b

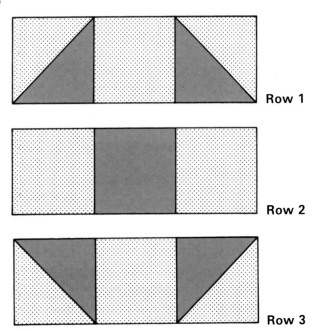

Row 1

Row 2

Row 3

5. Sew Rows 1, 2, and 3 together to complete Shoo Fly block *(Fig. 4c)*.

Fig. 4c

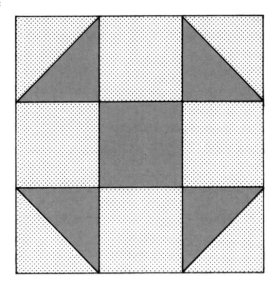

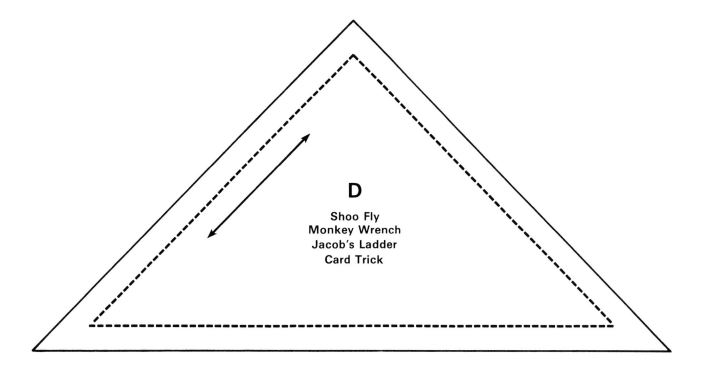

D

Shoo Fly
Monkey Wrench
Jacob's Ladder
Card Trick

Lesson Five

In this lesson you will make the **Monkey Wrench** block and gain more experience sewing triangles with bias edges together.

Fabric Key

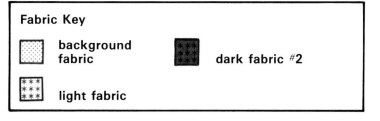

- background fabric
- dark fabric #2
- light fabric

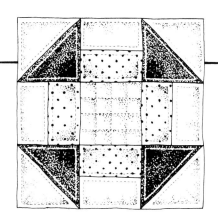

1. Make template E. You will also need templates C and D (previously made).
2. Cut out the following:
   - C — one from background fabric
   - D — four from background fabric
   - D — four from dark fabric #2
   - E — four from background fabric
   - E — four from light fabric
3. Sew one background fabric D to one dark fabric #2 D to make Unit 1 *(Fig. 5a)*. Repeat to make a total of four Unit 1's.

Fig. 5a

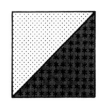

Unit 1

4. Sew one background fabric E to one light fabric E to make Unit 2 *(Fig. 5b)*. Repeat to make a total of four Unit 2's.

Fig. 5b

Unit 2

5. Sew one Unit 2 between two Unit 1's to make Row 1 *(Fig. 5c)*. Sew C between two Unit 2's to make Row 2. Sew one Unit 2 between two Unit 1's to make Row 3.

6. Sew Rows 1, 2, and 3 together to complete Monkey Wrench block *(Fig. 5d)*.

Fig. 5c

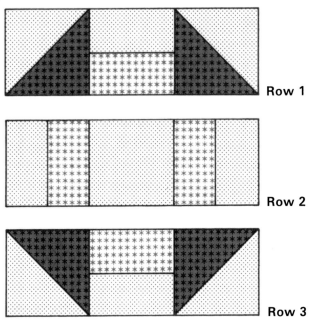

Row 1

Row 2

Row 3

Fig. 5d

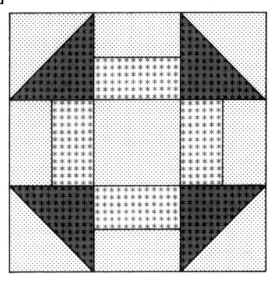

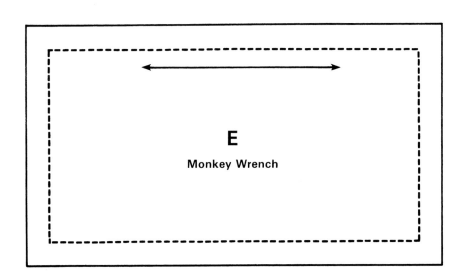

E

Monkey Wrench

Lesson Six

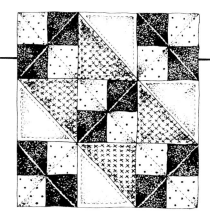

In this lesson you will make the **Jacob's Ladder** block and reinforce your piecing skills.

Fabric Key

 background fabric

medium fabric #2

 light fabric

dark fabric #2

1. Make template F. You will also need template D (previously made).
2. Cut out the following:
   D — four from background fabric
   D — four from medium fabric #2
   F — ten from light fabric
   F — ten from dark fabric #2
3. Sew one light fabric F to one dark fabric #2 F to make Unit 1 *(Fig. 6a)*. Repeat to make a total of ten Unit 1's.

Fig. 6a

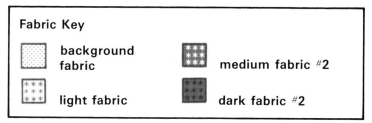 **Unit 1**

4. Sew two Unit 1's together to make Unit 2 *(Fig. 6b)*. Repeat to make a total of five Unit 2's.

Fig. 6b

 Unit 2

5. Sew one background fabric D to one medium fabric #2 D to make Unit 3 *(Fig. 6c)*. Repeat to make a total of four Unit 3's.

Fig. 6c

 Unit 3

6. Sew one Unit 3 between two Unit 2's to make Row 1 *(Fig. 6d)*. Sew one Unit 2 between two Unit 3's to make Row 2. Sew one Unit 3 between two Unit 2's to make Row 3.

Fig. 6d

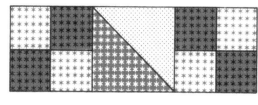 **Row 1**

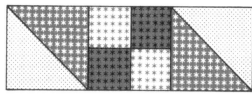 **Row 2**

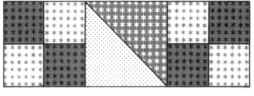 **Row 3**

7. Sew Rows 1, 2, and 3 together to complete Jacob's Ladder block *(Fig. 6e)*.

Fig. 6e

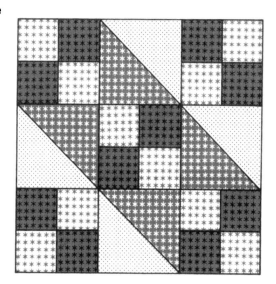

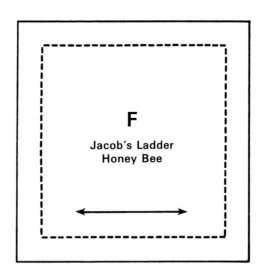

F

Jacob's Ladder
Honey Bee

Lesson Seven

In this lesson you will make the **Ohio Star** block and reinforce skills you have already learned.

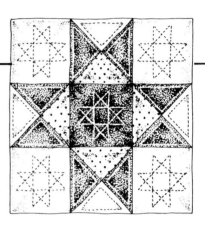

Fabric Key

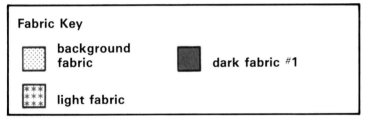

background fabric

dark fabric #1

light fabric

1. Make template G. You will also need template C (previously made).
2. Cut out the following:
   C — four from background fabric
   C — one from dark fabric #1
   G — four from background fabric
   G — four from light fabric
   G — eight from dark fabric #1
3. Sew one dark fabric #1 G to one background fabric G to make Unit 1 *(Fig. 7a)*. Repeat to make a total of four Unit 1's.

Fig. 7a

Unit 1

4. Sew one light fabric G to one dark fabric #1 G to make Unit 2 *(Fig. 7b)*. Repeat to make a total of four Unit 2's.

Fig. 7b

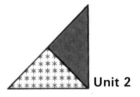

Unit 2

5. Sew one Unit 1 to one Unit 2 to make Unit 3 *(Fig. 7c)*. Repeat to make a total of four Unit 3's.

Fig. 7c

Unit 3

6. Sew one Unit 3 between two background fabric C's to make Row 1 *(Fig. 7d)*. Sew dark fabric #1 C between two Unit 3's to make Row 2. Sew one Unit 3 between two background fabric C's to make Row 3.

Fig. 7d

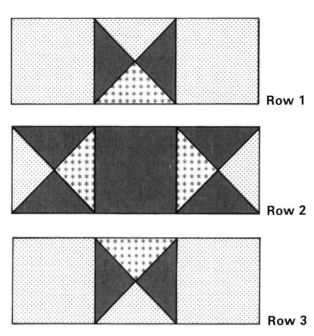

Row 1

Row 2

Row 3

7. Sew Rows 1, 2, and 3 together to complete Ohio Star block *(Fig. 7e)*.

Fig. 7e

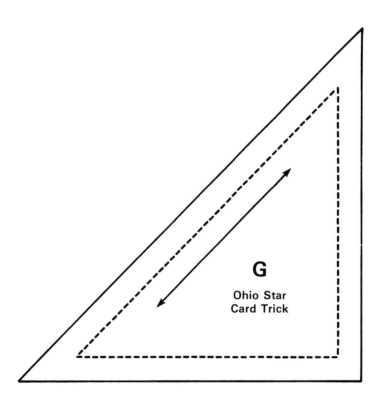

G

Ohio Star
Card Trick

Lesson Eight

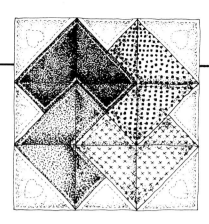

In this lesson you will make the **Card Trick** block and reinforce skills you have already learned.

Fabric Key

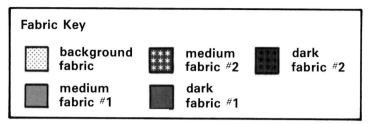

background fabric

medium fabric #1

medium fabric #2

dark fabric #1

dark fabric #2

1. You will need templates D and G (previously made).
2. Cut out the following:
   - D — four from background fabric
   - D — two from medium fabric #1
   - D — two from medium fabric #2
   - D — two from dark fabric #1
   - D — two from dark fabric #2
   - G — four from background fabric
   - G — two from medium fabric #1
   - G — two from medium fabric #2
   - G — two from dark fabric #1
   - G — two from dark fabric #2
3. Sew one background fabric D to one dark fabric #2 D to make Unit 1 *(Fig. 8a)*.

Fig. 8a

Unit 1

4. Sew one background fabric D to one medium fabric #1 D to make Unit 2 *(Fig. 8b)*.

Fig. 8b

Unit 2

5. Sew one background fabric D to one dark fabric #1 D to make Unit 3 *(Fig. 8c)*.

Fig. 8c

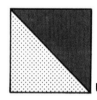

Unit 3

6. Sew one background fabric D to one medium fabric #2 D to make Unit 4 *(Fig. 8d)*.

Fig. 8d

Unit 4

7. Sew one background fabric G to one medium fabric #1 G to make Unit 5 *(Fig. 8e)*.

Fig. 8e

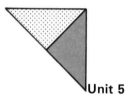

Unit 5

8. Sew one background fabric G to one medium fabric #2 G to make Unit 6 *(Fig. 8f)*.

Fig. 8f

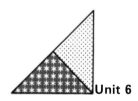

Unit 6

9. Sew one background fabric G to one dark fabric #1 G to make Unit 7 *(Fig. 8g)*.

Fig. 8g

Unit 7

10. Sew one background fabric G to one dark fabric #2 G to make Unit 8 *(Fig. 8h)*.

Fig. 8h

Unit 8

11. Sew one dark fabric #1 G to one dark fabric #2 G to make Unit 9 *(Fig. 8i)*.

Fig. 8i

Unit 9

12. Sew one medium fabric #1 G to one medium fabric #2 G to make Unit 10 *(Fig. 8j)*.

Fig. 8j

Unit 10

13. Sew Unit 9 to Unit 10 to make Unit 11 *(Fig. 8k)*.

Fig. 8k

Unit 11

14. Sew one dark fabric #2 D to Unit 5 to make Unit 12 *(Fig. 8l)*.

Fig. 8l

Unit 12

15. Sew one medium fabric #1 D to Unit 6 to make Unit 13 *(Fig. 8m)*.

Fig. 8m

Unit 13

16. Sew one medium fabric #2 D to Unit 7 to make Unit 14 *(Fig. 8n)*.

Fig. 8n

Unit 14

17. Sew one dark fabric #1 D to Unit 8 to make Unit 15 *(Fig. 8o)*.

Fig. 8o

Unit 15

18. Sew Unit 12 between Unit 1 and Unit 2 to make Row 1 *(Fig. 8p)*. Sew Unit 11 between Unit 15 and Unit 13 to make Row 2. Sew Unit 14 between Unit 3 and Unit 4 to make Row 3.

Fig. 8p

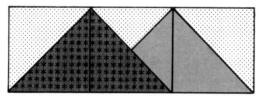

Row 1

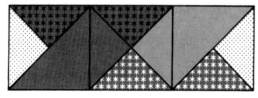

Row 2

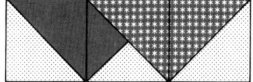

Row 3

18

19. Sew Rows 1, 2, and 3 together to complete Card Trick block *(Fig. 8q)*.

Fig. 8q

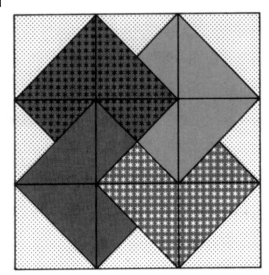

Lesson Nine

In this lesson, you will make the **Lily** block and reinforce skills you have already learned.

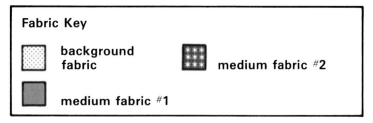

Fabric Key

☐ background fabric

☐ medium fabric #2

☐ medium fabric #1

1. Make templates H, I, J, K, and L.
2. Cut out the following:
   H — four from background fabric
   I — eight from background fabric
   I — eight from medium fabric #1
   J — four from medium fabric #2
   K — four from background fabric
   L — one from medium fabric #1
3. Sew one background fabric I to one medium fabric #1 I to make Unit 1 *(Fig. 9a)*. Repeat to make a total of four Unit 1's.

Fig. 9a

Unit 1

4. Sew one background fabric I to one medium fabric #1 I to make Unit 2 *(Fig. 9b)*. Repeat to make a total of four Unit 2's.

Fig. 9b

Unit 2

5. Sew one Unit 1 to one H *(Fig. 9c)*. Sew one Unit 2 to same H to make Unit 3 *(Fig. 9d)*. Repeat to make a total of four Unit 3's.

Fig. 9c

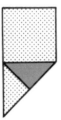

Fig. 9d

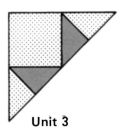

Unit 3

6. Sew one J to one Unit 3 to make Unit 4 *(Fig. 9e)*. Repeat to make a total of four Unit 4's.

Fig. 9e

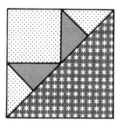

Unit 4

7. Sew one K between two Unit 4's to make Row 1 *(Fig. 9f)*. Sew L between two K's to make Row 2. Sew one K between two Unit 4's to make Row 3.

Fig. 9f

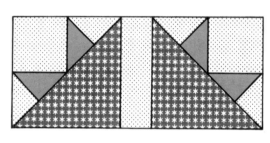

Row 1

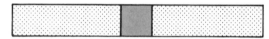

Row 2

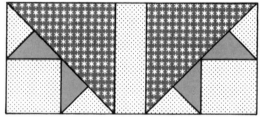

Row 3

8. Sew Rows 1, 2, and 3 together to complete Lily block *(Fig. 9g)*.

Fig. 9g

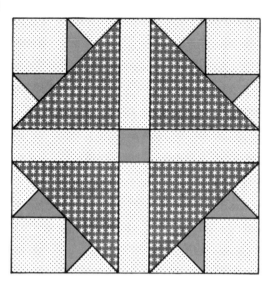

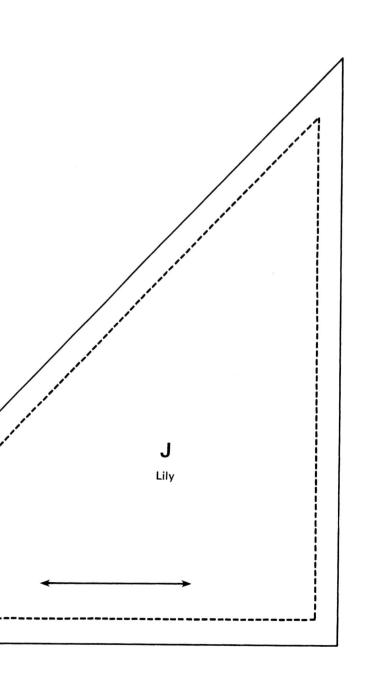

J

Lily

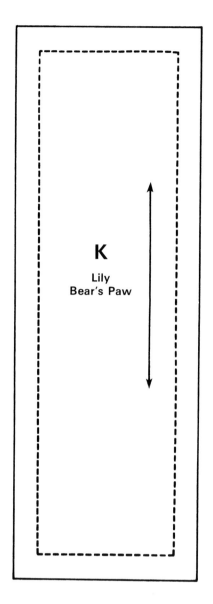

K

Lily
Bear's Paw

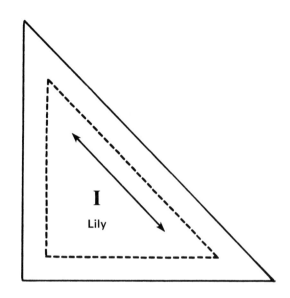

I

Lily

L

Lily
Star In A Star
Bear's Paw

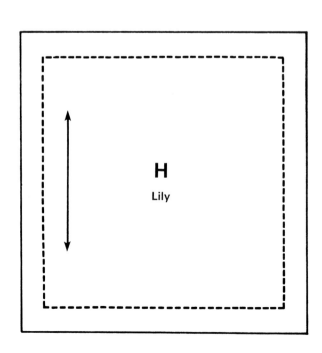

H

Lily

21

Lesson Ten

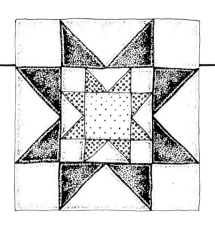

In this lesson, you will make the **Star In A Star** block and learn to sew together pieces that do not match exactly.

Fabric Key

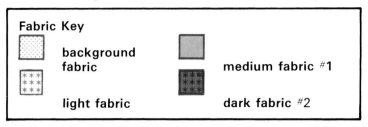

background fabric

light fabric

medium fabric #1

dark fabric #2

1. Make templates M, N, O, P, and Q. You will also need template L (previously made). *(Note: If machine piecing, remember that when patterns have dots, it is important to transfer them to your templates and to fabric pieces. These are important when sewing together pieces with edges that do not match exactly. If hand piecing, continue to mark and follow sewing line as usual.)*

2. Cut out the following:
   - L — four from background fabric
   - M — four from background fabric
   - M — one from light fabric
   - N — eight from dark fabric #2
   - O — four from background fabric
   - P — eight from medium fabric #1
   - Q — four from background fabric

3. Referring to **Figs. 10a-10b**, pin and sew one N to one O. *(Note: If machine piecing, match dots when pinning pieces together. However, you may sew from fabric edge to fabric edge and not just between the dots when joining these pieces.)*

Fig. 10a

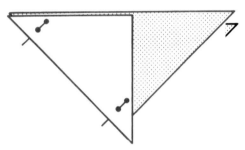

Fig. 10b

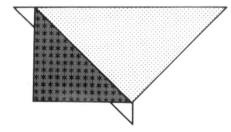

4. Sew one N to same O to make Unit 1 *(Fig. 10c)*. Repeat to make a total of four Unit 1's.

Fig. 10c

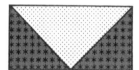

Unit 1

5. Sew one P to one Q; sew one P to same Q to make Unit 2 *(Fig. 10d)*. Repeat to make a total of four Unit 2's.

Fig. 10d

Unit 2

6. Sew one Unit 2 between two L's to make Unit 3 *(Fig. 10e)*. Repeat to make a total of two Unit 3's.

Fig. 10e

Unit 3

7. Sew light fabric M between two Unit 2's to make Unit 4 *(Fig. 10f)*.

Fig. 10f

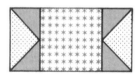

Unit 4

8. Sew Unit 4 between two Unit 3's to make Unit 5 *(Fig. 10g)*.

Fig. 10g

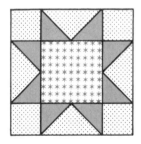

Unit 5

9. Sew one Unit 1 between two M's to make Row 1 *(Fig. 10h)*. Sew Unit 5 between two Unit 1's to make Row 2. Sew one Unit 1 between two M's to make Row 3.

10. Sew Rows 1, 2, and 3 together to complete Star In A Star block *(Fig. 10i)*.

Fig. 10i

Fig. 10h

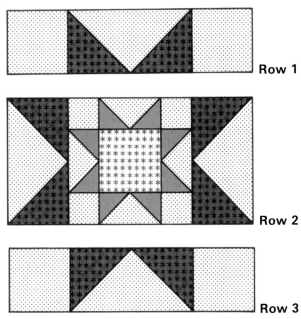

Row 1

Row 2

Row 3

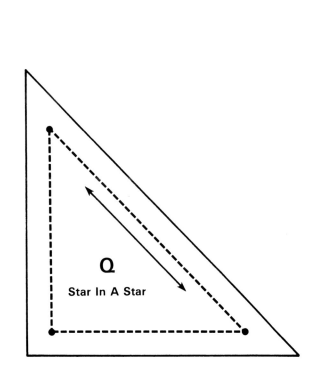

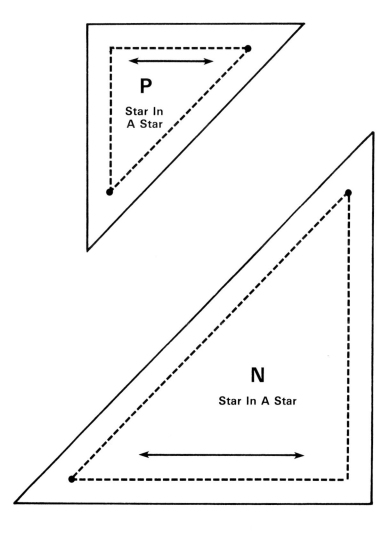

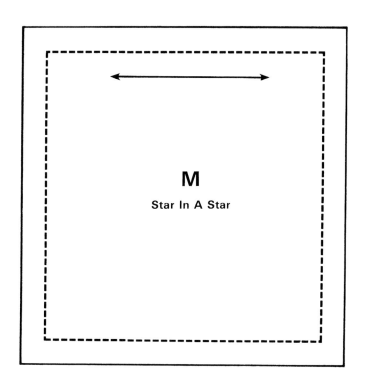

M

Star In A Star

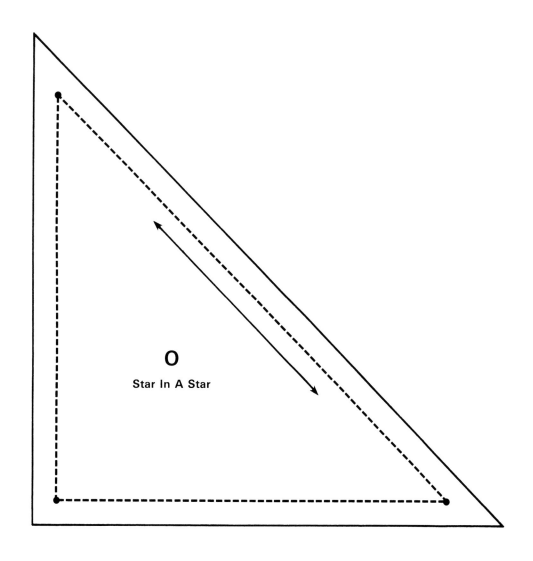

O

Star In A Star

Lesson Eleven _____

In this lesson, you will make the **Wedding Ring** block and reinforce skills you have already learned.

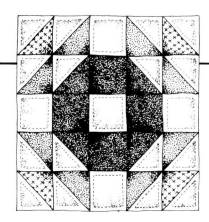

Fabric Key

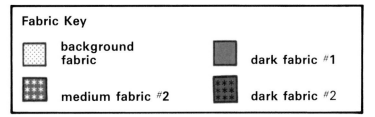

| | background fabric | | dark fabric #1 |
| | medium fabric #2 | | dark fabric #2 |

1. Make templates R and S.
2. Cut out the following:
   R — sixteen from background fabric
   R — four from medium fabric #2
   R — eight from dark fabric #1
   R — four from dark fabric #2
   S — five from background fabric
   S — four from dark fabric #2
3. Sew one background fabric R to one medium fabric #2 R to make Unit 1 *(Fig. 11a)*. Repeat to make a total of four Unit 1's.

Fig. 11a

 Unit 1

4. Sew one background fabric R to one dark fabric #1 R to make Unit 2 *(Fig. 11b)*. Repeat to make a total of eight Unit 2's.

Fig. 11b

 Unit 2

5. Sew one background fabric R to one dark fabric #2 R to make Unit 3 *(Fig. 11c)*. Repeat to make a total of four Unit 3's.

Fig. 11c

 Unit 3

6. Sew one background fabric S between two Unit 2's to make Unit 4 *(Fig. 11d)*. Sew Unit 4 between two Unit 1's to make Row 1 *(Fig. 11e)*.

Fig. 11d

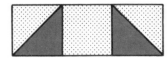 Unit 4

Fig. 11e

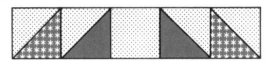 Row 1

7. Sew one dark fabric #2 S between two Unit 3's to make Unit 5 *(Fig. 11f)*. Sew Unit 5 between two Unit 2's to make Row 2 *(Fig. 11g)*.

Fig. 11f

 Unit 5

Fig. 11g

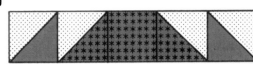 Row 2

8. Sew one background fabric S between two dark fabric #2 S's to make Unit 6 *(Fig. 11h)*. Sew Unit 6 between two background fabric S's to make Row 3 *(Fig. 11i)*.

Fig. 11h

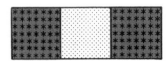 Unit 6

Fig. 11i

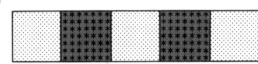 Row 3

9. Repeat Step 7 to make Row 4 *(Fig. 11j)*.

Fig. 11j

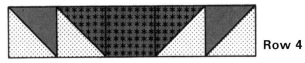

Row 4

10. Repeat Step 6 to make Row 5 *(Fig. 11k)*.

Fig. 11k

Row 5

11. Sew Rows 1-5 together to complete Wedding Ring block *(Fig. 11l)*.

Fig. 11l

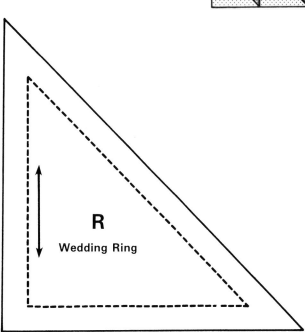

R
Wedding Ring

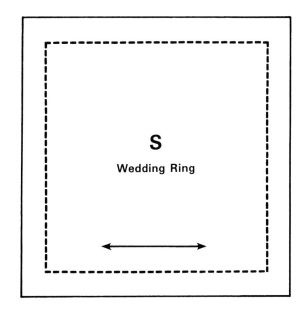

S
Wedding Ring

Lesson Twelve

In this lesson you will make the **Bear's Paw** block and reinforce skills you have already learned.

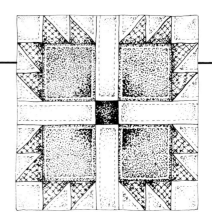

Fabric Key

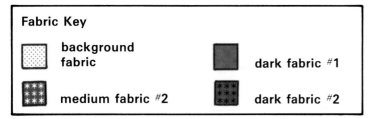

background fabric

dark fabric #1

medium fabric #2

dark fabric #2

1. Make templates T, U, and V. You will also need templates K and L (previously made). *(Note: Transfer dots to template V. The dots do not need to be transferred to fabric pieces for this block, but they will need to be transferred to fabric pieces for the LeMoyne Star block.)*

2. Cut out the following:
   K — four from background fabric
   L — one from dark fabric #2
   T — four from background fabric
   U — sixteen from background fabric
   U — sixteen from medium fabric #2
   V — four from dark fabric #1

3. Sew one background fabric U to one medium fabric #2 U to make Unit 1 *(Fig. 12a)*. Repeat to make a total of sixteen Unit 1's.

Fig. 12a

 Unit 1

4. Sew two Unit 1's together to make Unit 2 *(Fig. 12b)*. Repeat to make a total of four Unit 2's.

Fig. 12b

 Unit 2

5. Sew two Unit 1's together to make Unit 3 *(Fig. 12c)*. Repeat to make a total of four Unit 3's.

Fig. 12c

 Unit 3

6. Sew one T to one Unit 2 to make Unit 4 *(Fig. 12d)*. Repeat to make a total of four Unit 4's.

Fig. 12d

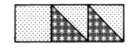 Unit 4

7. Sew one Unit 3 to one V to make Unit 5 *(Fig. 12e)*. Repeat to make a total of four Unit 5's.

Fig. 12e

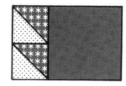 Unit 5

8. Sew one Unit 4 to one Unit 5 to make Unit 6 *(Fig. 12f)*. Repeat to make a total of four Unit 6's.

Fig. 12f

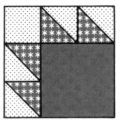 Unit 6

9. Sew one K between two Unit 6's to make Row 1 *(Fig. 12g)*. Sew L between two K's to make Row 2. Sew one K between two Unit 6's to make Row 3.

Fig. 12g

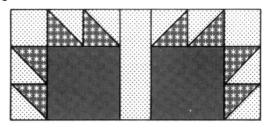 Row 1

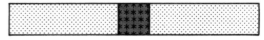 Row 2

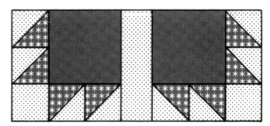 Row 3

10. Sew Rows 1, 2, and 3 together to complete Bear's Paw
    block *(Fig. 12h)*.

Fig. 12h

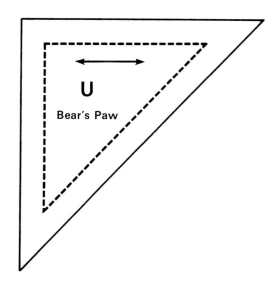

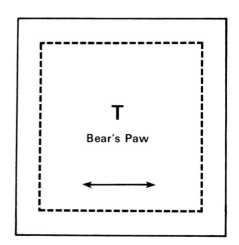

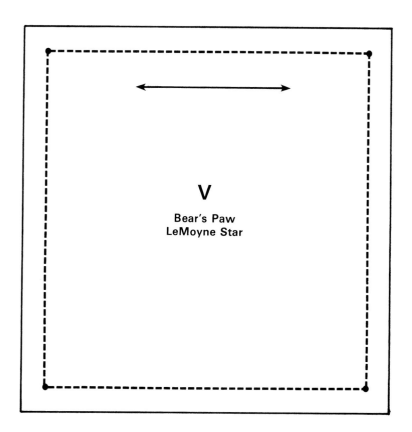

Lesson Thirteen

In this lesson you will make the **Drunkard's Path** block and learn to sew pieces with curved edges together.

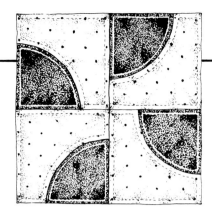

Fabric Key

light fabric   dark fabric #2

---

1. Make templates W and X.
2. Cut out the following:
   W — four from light fabric
   X — four from dark fabric #2
3. Follow **Sewing Curves** to sew one W to one X to make Unit 1 *(Fig. 13a)*. Repeat to make a total of four Unit 1's.

Fig. 13a

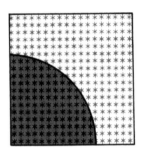

Unit 1

SEWING CURVES

It is important that you mark center of edges on curved pieces as indicated on patterns. Clip curved edge of piece W to make pinning easier. Place pieces right sides together matching centers *(Fig. 13b)*. Pin curved edges together at center and corners *(Fig. 13c)*; pin edges together between center and corners, easing in fullness as shown in **Fig. 13d**. Sew pieces together along the curved seamline. *(**Note:** In hand piecing, make sure you sew through the drawn line on both pieces.)*

Fig. 13b

Fig. 13c

Fig. 13d

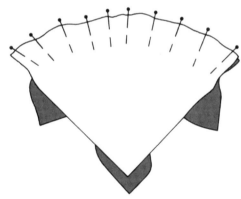

4. Sew two Unit 1's together to make Row 1 *(Fig. 13e)*. Sew two Unit 1's together to make Row 2.

29

Fig. 13e

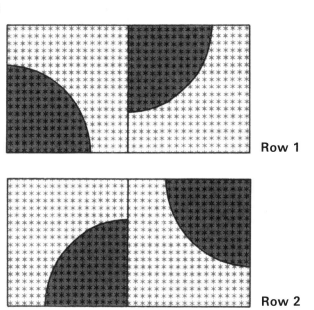

Row 1

Row 2

5. Sew Rows 1 and 2 together to complete Drunkard's Path block *(Fig. 13f)*.

Fig. 13f

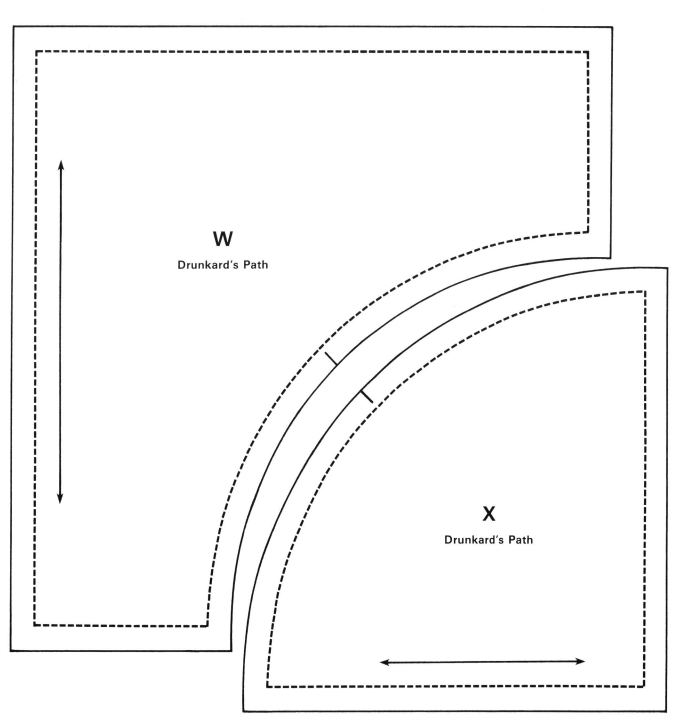

W

Drunkard's Path

X

Drunkard's Path

Lesson Fourteen

In this lesson you will make the **Basket** block. You will learn about reversing a template and learn the two appliqué stitches. You will also learn how to press appliquéd blocks.

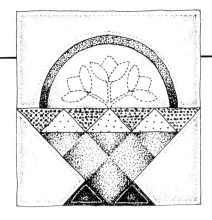

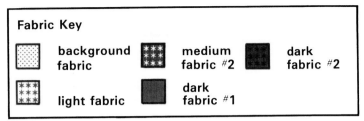

Fabric Key

☐	background fabric	▦	medium fabric #2	■	dark fabric #2
▦	light fabric	■	dark fabric #1		

1. Make templates Y, Z, AA, and BB. *(Note: Trace placement lines onto template Y.)*
2. Cut out the following:
   Y — one from background fabric (cut on fold)
   Z — three from light fabric
   Z — four from medium fabric #2
   Z — two from dark fabric #2
   AA — one from dark fabric #1
   BB — one from background fabric; one in reverse from background fabric
3. For basket handle, cut a 1¾" x 15" bias strip from dark fabric #1.
4. With **wrong** sides together, use a ¼" seam allowance to sew long raw edges of strip together *(Fig. 14a)*.

Fig. 14a

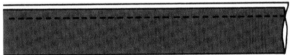

5. Center seam along back of strip and **lightly** press seam allowances to one side *(Fig. 14b)*.

Fig. 14b

6. To mark placement lines for basket handle on right side of fabric piece Y, place template Y under fabric and trace placement lines to half of fabric. If using a plastic template, turn template over to transfer placement lines to remaining half of fabric. If not, make a template Y from typing paper and use a #2 pencil to trace placement lines to opposite side of paper. Place paper under fabric and trace placement lines to remaining half of fabric.
7. Using placement lines as a guide, carefully pin handle, right side up, to background fabric. *(Note: The handle is cut extra long to allow for fit; ends will extend beyond fabric edge. Also, remember to use sequin pins or trim pins when pinning appliqués in place.)*
8. Sewing inside of curve first, use **Appliqué Stitch A** or **B** to appliqué handle to background fabric to make Row 1. Trim handle ends even with raw edge of background fabric *(Fig. 14c)*.

Fig. 14c

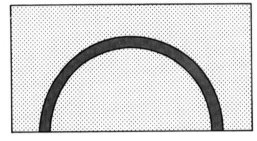

Row 1

APPLIQUÉ STITCHES

There are two appliqué stitches commonly used by quilters. **Appliqué Stitch A** is an invisible stitch and is preferred by many quilters. **Appliqué Stitch B** is a more traditional stitch with a small amount of thread showing on the appliqué. Try both techniques and use the one you prefer. Match color of thread to color of appliqué; this will help disguise your stitches. Thread appliqué needle with a 20-24" length of sewing thread; knot one end. Stitches should be approximately 1/16" apart and never longer than 1/8".

Appliqué Stitch A

Bring needle up through background fabric at 1 *(Fig. 14d)*; needle should come up even with edge of appliqué. Insert needle in folded edge of appliqué at 2, directly across from 1; bring needle out of folded edge at 3 *(Fig. 14e)*. Insert needle into background fabric at 4, even with edge of appliqué and directly across from 3; bring needle back up through background fabric at 5 *(Fig. 14f)*, forming a small stitch on wrong side of fabric. Stitches on right side of fabric should not show. Stitches in folded edge of appliqué and on background fabric should be equal in length. Repeat stitches as shown in **Figs. 14e** and **14f** until you have completely secured edge of appliqué in place. Secure and clip thread.

Fig. 14d

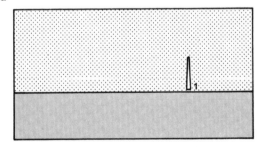

Fig. 14e

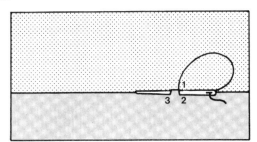

Fig. 14f

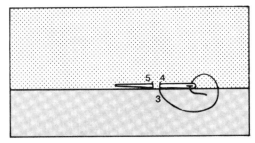

Appliqué Stitch B

Bring needle up into edge of appliqué at 1, catching two or three threads of appliqué *(Fig. 14g)*. Insert needle into background fabric at 2, directly across from 1 *(Fig. 14h)*. Bring needle up at 3 into edge of appliqué and down at 4 into background fabric *(Fig. 14i)*. Continue stitching in this manner *(Fig. 14j)* until you have completely secured edge of appliqué in place. Secure and clip thread.

Fig. 14g

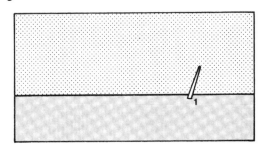

Fig. 14h

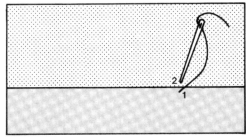

Fig. 14i

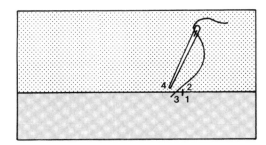

Fig. 14j

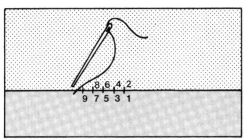

9. Referring to **Figs. 14k** and **14l**, pin and sew one medium fabric #2 Z to one light fabric Z. *(**Note:** If machine piecing, match dots when pinning pieces together. However, you may sew from fabric edge to fabric edge and not just between the dots when joining these pieces.)*

Fig. 14k

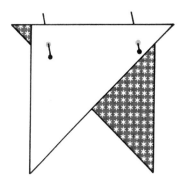

Fig. 14l

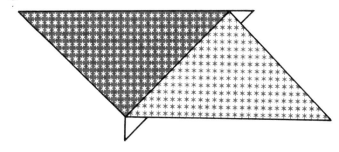

10. Add medium fabric #2 Z's and light fabric Z's to make Unit 1 *(Fig. 14m)*.

Fig. 14m

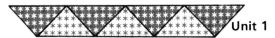

Unit 1

11. Sew AA to Unit 1 to make Unit 2 *(Fig. 14n)*. *(**Note:** When pinning these pieces together, it may be helpful to pin ends and centers; then, ease in fullness between pins.)*

Fig. 14n

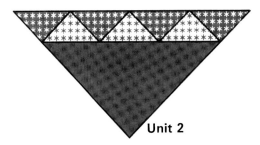

Unit 2

12. Sew BB to one Z to make Unit 3 *(Fig. 14o)*.

Fig. 14o

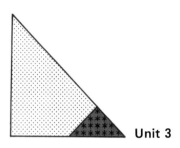

Unit 3

13. Sew reverse BB to remaining Z to make Unit 4 *(Fig. 14p)*.

Fig. 14p

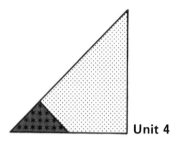

Unit 4

14. Sew Unit 3 to Unit 2 *(Fig. 14q)*. Sew Unit 4 to Unit 2 to make Row 2 *(Fig. 14r)*.

Fig. 14q

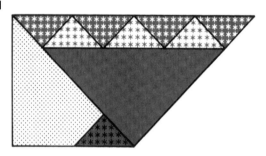

Fig. 14r

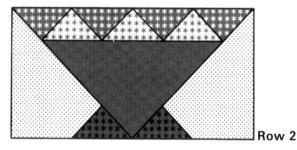

Row 2

15. Sew Rows 1 and 2 together to complete Basket block *(Fig. 14s)*.

Fig. 14s

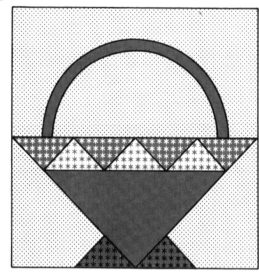

16. Follow **Pressing Appliquéd Blocks** to press block.

PRESSING APPLIQUÉD BLOCKS
To prevent distorting appliqués when pressing blocks with appliquéd shapes, place a towel on ironing board and place the block face down on the towel. Press block from wrong side.

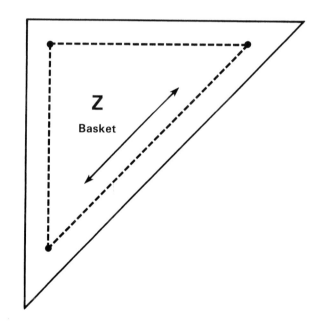

Z

Basket

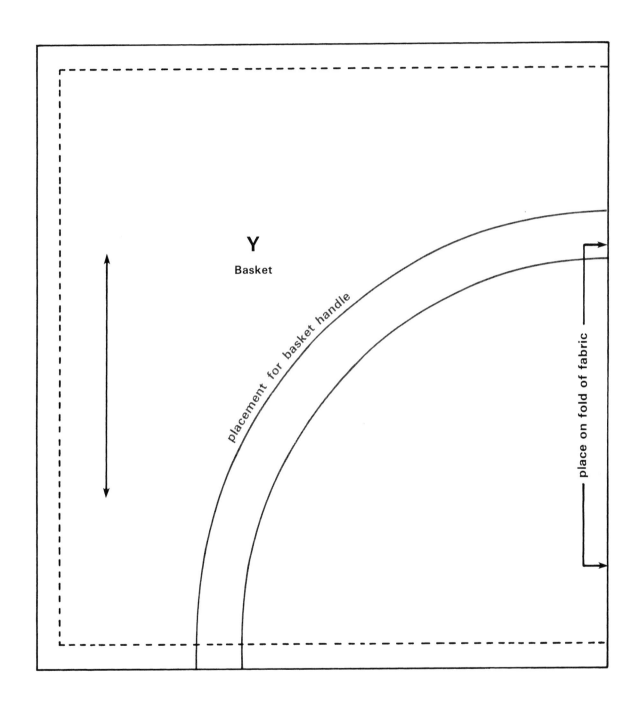

Y

Basket

placement for basket handle

place on fold of fabric

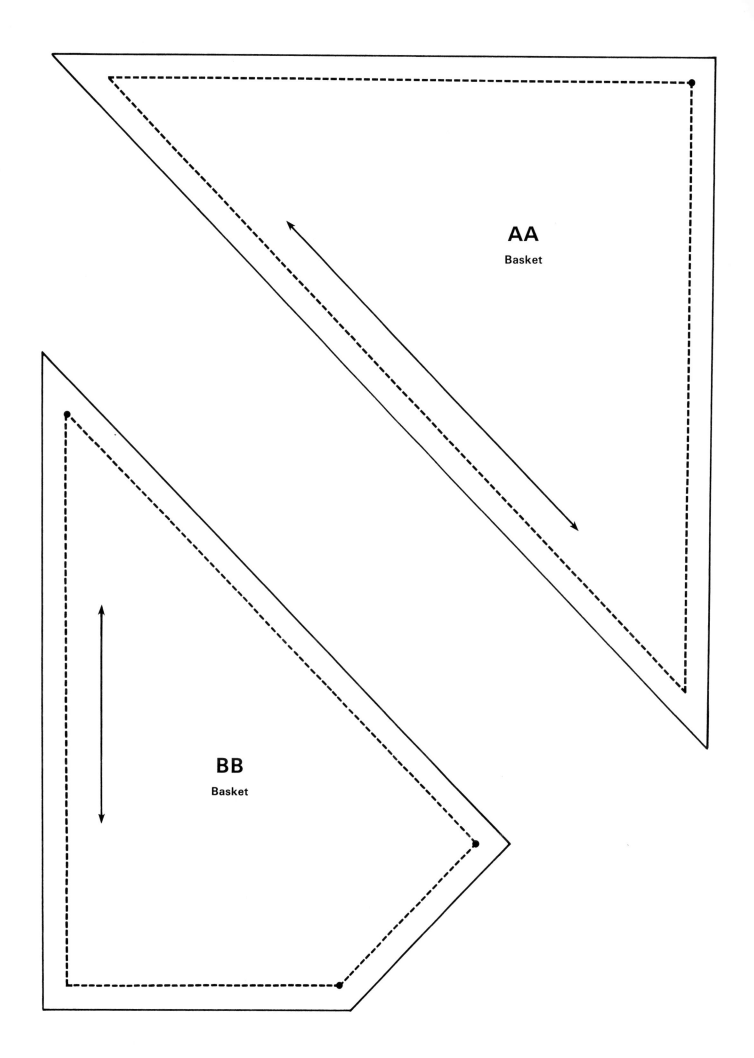

AA

Basket

BB

Basket

Lesson Fifteen

In this lesson you will make the **Grandma's Fan** block and practice sewing curved edges together.

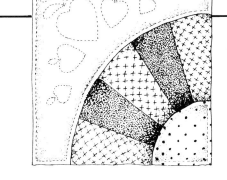

	Fabric Key		
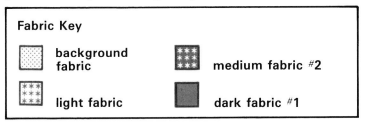			

background fabric

light fabric

medium fabric #2

dark fabric #1

1. Make templates CC, DD, and EE. *(**Note:** If using clear plastic sheets for templates, trace quilting lines onto template EE.)*
2. Cut out the following:
   CC — three from medium fabric #2
   CC — two from dark fabric #1
   DD — one from light fabric
   EE — one from background fabric (cut on fold)
3. Sew CC's together to make Unit 1 *(Fig. 15a)*.

Fig. 15a

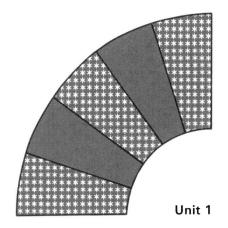

Unit 1

4. Sew DD to Unit 1 *(Fig. 15b)*. *(**Note:** When preparing to sew pieces together in this step and Step 5, clip the inner curved edge and pin pieces together at center and ends, then pin remainder of edge.)*

Fig. 15b

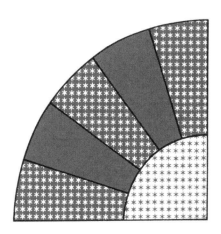

5. Sew EE to Unit 1 to complete Grandma's Fan block *(Fig. 15c)*.

Fig. 15c

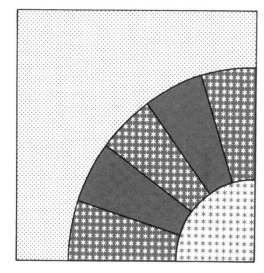

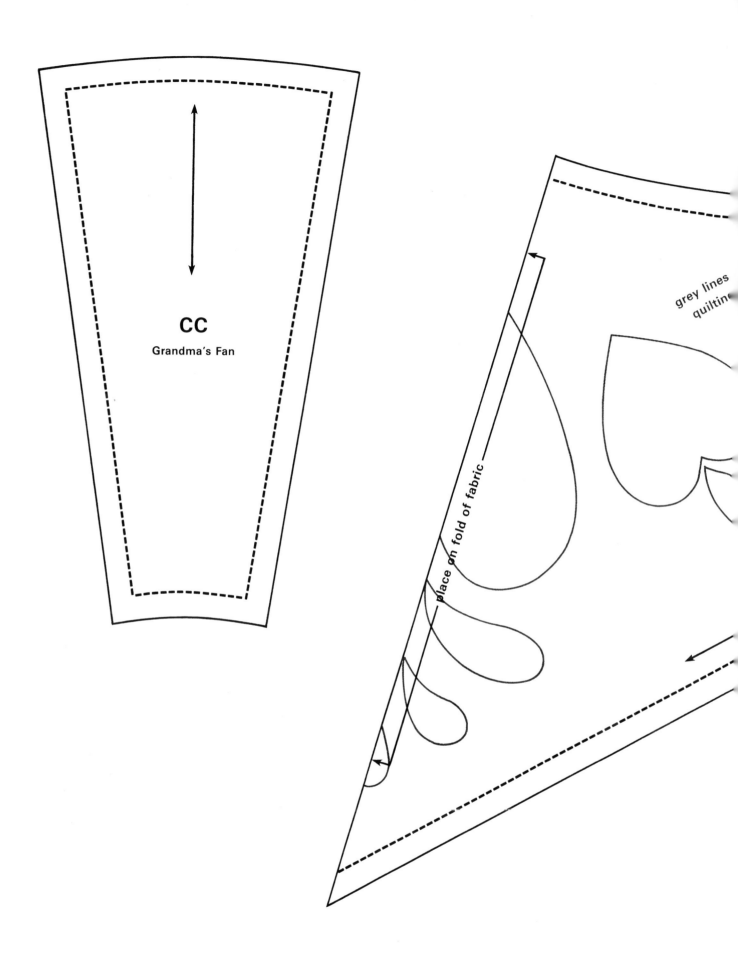

CC

Grandma's Fan

place on fold of fabric

grey lines
quiltin

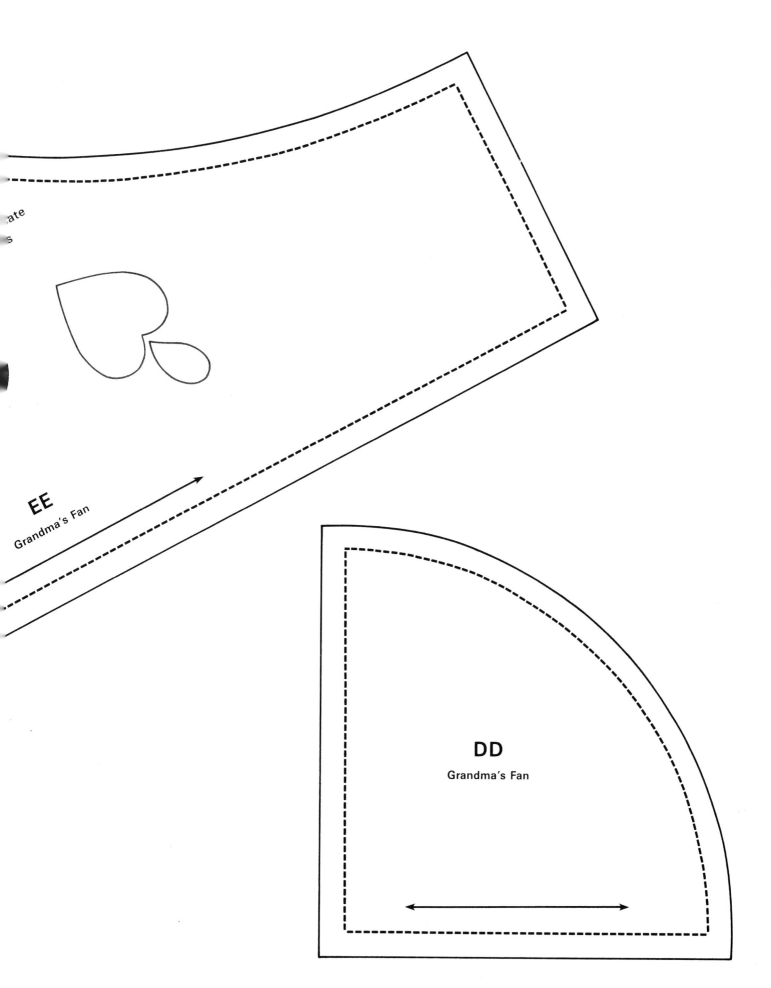

EE

Grandma's Fan

DD

Grandma's Fan

Lesson Sixteen

In this lesson you will make the **Spring Bloom** block and learn the Simple Basting Appliqué Method. You will also learn about cutting away fabric behind an appliqué.

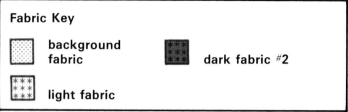
1. Make templates FF and GG. (**Note:** *These patterns do not include seam allowances. Seam allowances will be added when fabric pieces are cut out.*)
2. Cut a 12½" square from background fabric.
3. Fold background fabric in half from top to bottom; finger press and unfold. Fold in half from left to right; finger press and unfold.
4. Using fold lines as a guide, place one quarter of fabric right side up over Placement Diagram on pg. 41 and use marking tool to lightly trace placement lines. Repeat for each quarter of fabric. (**Note:** *Use a light table or sunny window, if necessary, in order to see lines through fabric.*)
5. Follow the **Simple Basting Appliqué Method** to make four dark fabric #2 petals (FF) and one light fabric center (GG); appliqué shapes to background fabric to complete Spring Bloom block (**Fig. 16a**).

Fig. 16a

SIMPLE BASTING APPLIQUÉ METHOD

This method involves basting the seam allowance of the appliqué in place before the appliqué is positioned on the background fabric.

1. Place template on **right** side of appliqué fabric.
2. Use a marking tool to draw around template. Leaving at least ½" between shapes, repeat for number of shapes specified. Cut out each shape approximately ³⁄₁₆" outside drawn line. Clip inward point at top of each petal up to, but not through, drawn line (**Fig. 16b**).

Fig. 16b

3. Thread appliqué needle with a single strand of sewing thread; knot one end.
4. For each appliqué shape, begin on as straight an edge as possible and turn a small section of seam allowance to wrong side with your fingers, concealing the drawn line. Use a Running Stitch to baste seam allowance in place (**Fig. 16c**). (**Note:** *Do not turn seam allowance at bottom edge of petal to wrong side; the center piece will cover this edge.*)

Fig. 16c

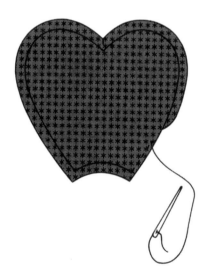

5. Continue basting around shape. When basting curves, work a small area at a time; you may even need to take one stitch at a time on curves to gently ease in fullness.

6. When all shapes have been basted, use placement lines as a guide to pin shapes to background fabric. (**Note:** *When pinning center piece in place, match straight grain or design of appliqué fabric to straight grain of background fabric.)*

7. Use **Appliqué Stitch A** or **B** to appliqué shapes to fabric, appliquéing petals first. Remove basting thread and pins from each appliqué shape.

8. Follow **Cutting Away Fabric Behind Appliqués** to reduce bulk behind appliqués.

CUTTING AWAY FABRIC BEHIND APPLIQUÉS

Quilting an appliquéd block will be easier if you are stitching through as few layers as possible. For this reason, or just to reduce bulk in your quilt, you may want to cut away the background fabric behind the appliqués. After stitching the appliqués in place, turn the block over. Use sharp scissors to trim away the background fabric to approximately $\frac{3}{16}$" from sewing line (**Fig. 16d**); take care not to cut appliqué fabric or any stitches.

Fig. 16d

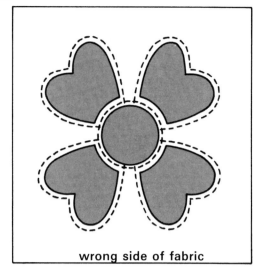

wrong side of fabric

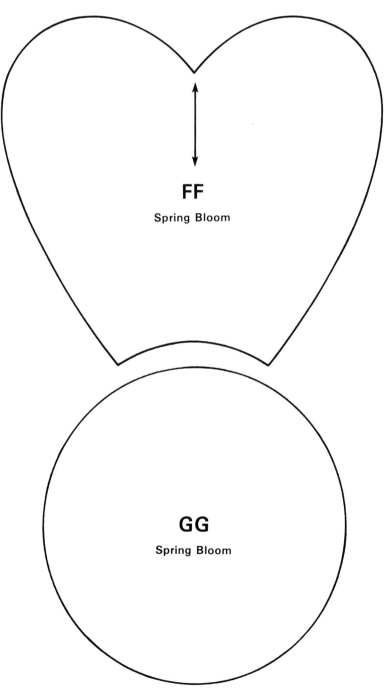

FF

Spring Bloom

GG

Spring Bloom

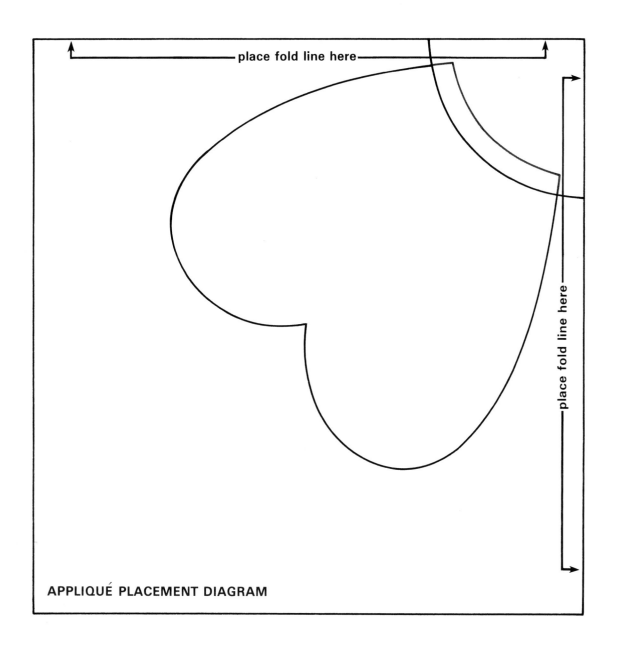

place fold line here

place fold line here

APPLIQUÉ PLACEMENT DIAGRAM

Lesson Seventeen

In this lesson you will make the **Honey Bee** block and learn the Paper Basting Appliqué Method.

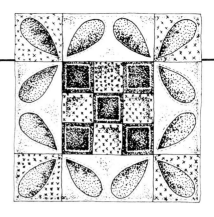

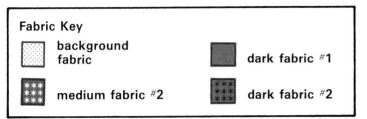

Fabric Key

background fabric

dark fabric #1

medium fabric #2

dark fabric #2

1. Make templates HH and II. You will also need template F (previously made). Paper templates for JJ pieces will be made in Step 9.
2. Cut out the following:
   F — four from medium fabric #2
   F — five from dark fabric #2
   HH — four from medium fabric #2
   II — four from background fabric
3. Sew one medium fabric #2 F between two dark fabric #2 F's to make Unit 1 *(Fig. 17a)*. Repeat to make a total of two Unit 1's.

Fig. 17a

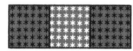

Unit 1

4. Sew one dark fabric #2 F between two medium fabric #2 F's to make Unit 2 *(Fig. 17b)*.

Fig. 17b

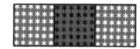

Unit 2

5. Sew Unit 2 between Unit 1's to make Unit 3 *(Fig. 17c)*.

Fig. 17c

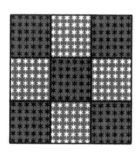

Unit 3

6. Sew one II between two HH's to make Row 1 *(Fig. 17d)*. Sew Unit 3 between two II's to make Row 2. Sew one II between two HH's to make Row 3.

Fig. 17d

Row 1

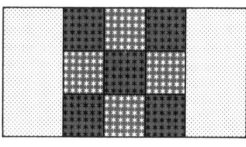

Row 2

Row 3

7. Sew Rows 1, 2, and 3 together *(Fig. 17e)*.

Fig. 17e

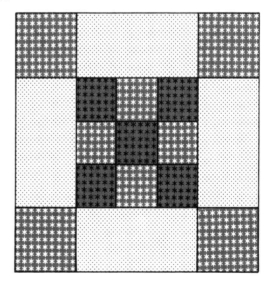

8. To transfer placement lines for appliqué pieces, place fabric right side up over patterns HH and II; use marking tool to lightly trace placement lines onto fabric.

9. Follow the **Paper Basting Appliqué Method** to make twelve dark fabric #1 wings (JJ); appliqué wings to fabric to complete Honey Bee block *(Fig. 17f)*.

Fig. 17f

PAPER BASTING APPLIQUE METHOD

This method prepares a shape to be appliquéd by basting the seam allowance over a paper template.

1. Place a piece of typing paper over appliqué pattern (JJ). Trace pattern and cut out directly on drawn line. You will need a separate paper template for each appliqué shape in the design. For the Honey Bee, you will need twelve ''wings.''

2. Place paper template on wrong side of appliqué fabric and draw around template. Cut out shape leaving an approximate ¼" seam allowance *(Fig. 17g)*. Repeat for each appliqué shape.

Fig. 17g

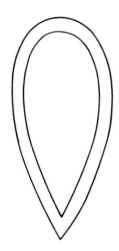

3. Center paper template on wrong side of fabric shape; pin in place.

4. Thread appliqué needle with a single strand of sewing thread; knot one end.

5. Holding template and fabric with your nonstitching hand and beginning on as straight an edge as possible, fold a small section of seam allowance over edge of paper.

6. Use a Running Stitch to baste seam allowance in place, stitching **through** paper *(Fig. 17h)*. Working a small amount of seam allowance at a time, continue basting around shape.

Fig. 17h

7. For outward point, fold seam allowance over template at point as shown in **Fig. 17i**.

Fig. 17i

8. Fold seam allowance over template on one side of point and baste to point *(Fig. 17j)*.

9. Fold seam allowance over on opposite side of point and finish basting *(Fig. 17k)*.

Fig. 17j   **Fig. 17k**

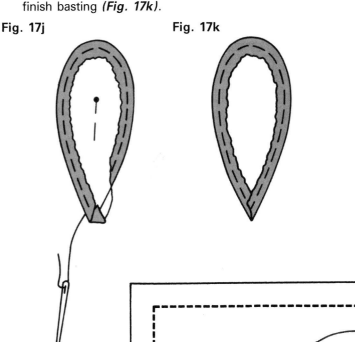

10. When all shapes have been basted, use placement lines as a guide and pin shapes right side up on fabric.

11. Use **Appliqué Stitch A** or **B** to appliqué shapes to fabric. Remove basting thread and pins from each appliqué shape.

12. Turn block over. Use sharp scissors to trim away the background fabric behind each appliqué to approximately $\frac{3}{16}''$ from sewing line *(Fig. 17l)*; take care not to cut appliqué fabric or any stitches. Remove paper from appliqué shape.

Fig. 17l

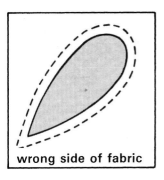

wrong side of fabric

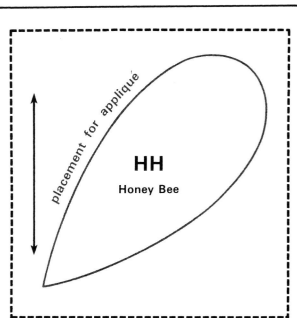

placement for appliqué

HH
Honey Bee

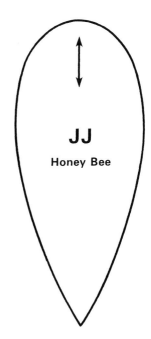

JJ
Honey Bee

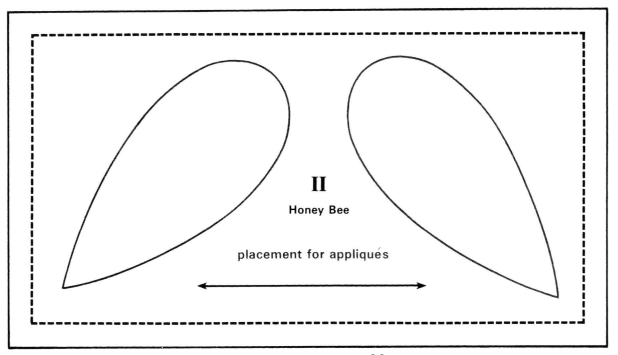

II
Honey Bee

placement for appliqués

44

Lesson Eighteen

In this lesson you will make the **Friendship Star** block and learn a third appliqué method, Needle Turning.

Fabric Key

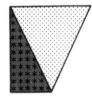	background fabric	▨	dark fabric #1
▨	medium fabric #2	▨	dark fabric #2

1. Make templates KK, LL, MM, and NN. *(Note: Pattern NN does not include seam allowance. Seam allowance will be added when fabric piece is cut out.)*
2. Cut out the following:
   KK — four from background fabric
   KK — one from medium fabric #2
   LL — four from dark fabric #2; four in reverse from dark fabric #2
   MM — four from background fabric
3. Sew one LL to one MM *(Fig. 18a)*. *(Note: If machine piecing, match dots when pinning pieces together. However, you may sew from fabric edge to fabric edge and not just between the dots when joining these pieces.)* Sew one reverse LL to same MM to make Unit 1 *(Fig. 18b)*. Repeat to make a total of four Unit 1's.

Fig. 18a   **Fig. 18b**

Unit 1

4. Sew one Unit 1 between two background fabric KK's to make Row 1 *(Fig. 18c)*. Sew medium fabric #2 KK between two Unit 1's to make Row 2. Sew one Unit 1 between two background fabric KK's to make Row 3.

Fig. 18c

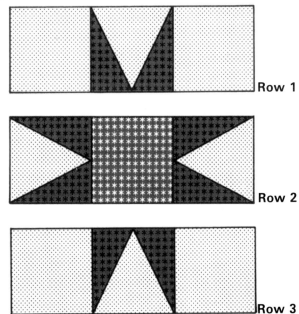

Row 1

Row 2

Row 3

5. Sew Rows 1, 2, and 3 together *(Fig. 18d)*.

Fig. 18d

6. To mark placement for heart on center square, place fabric over pattern KK and trace heart onto fabric.
7. Follow the **Needle Turn Appliqué Method** to make one heart (NN) from dark fabric #1; appliqué heart to fabric to complete Friendship Star block *(Fig. 18e)*.

Fig. 18e

NEEDLE TURN APPLIQUÉ METHOD

In this method the seam allowance of the appliqué is not basted before the appliqué is pinned to the background fabric. The needle is used to turn the seam allowance to the wrong side as the shape is appliquéd in place.

1. Place template on **right** side of appliqué fabric and draw around template.
2. Trim fabric approximately ³⁄₁₆" outside drawn line. Clip inward point at top of heart up to, but not through, drawn line.
3. Using placement line as a guide, pin appliqué shape to background fabric *(Fig. 18f)*.

Fig. 18f

4. Thread appliqué needle with a single strand of sewing thread; knot one end.
5. Beginning on as straight an edge as possible, use the point of your needle to turn a small section of the seam allowance under, concealing the drawn line *(Fig. 18g)*. Use **Appliqué Stitch A** or **B** to secure fold of appliqué to background fabric.

Fig. 18g

6. Working a small section of seam allowance at a time, appliqué around heart until you are approximately ½" from outward point *(Fig. 18h)*.

Fig. 18h

7. Turn seam allowance under at point as shown in **Fig. 18i.**

Fig. 18i

8. Turning seam allowance under and using your nonstitching hand to hold it in place, stitch to point, bringing needle up into fabric directly at point *(Fig. 18j)*. Take two or three stitches at point to secure.

Fig. 18j

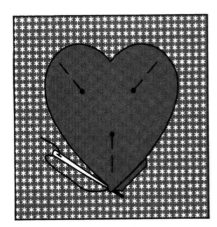

9. Turn under a small amount of seam allowance past point and resume appliquéing **(Fig. 18k)**.

Fig. 18k

10. The appliqué on this block will not be quilted; however, if you wish to reduce bulk, trim background fabric behind the appliqué in the same manner as previous appliquéd blocks were trimmed.

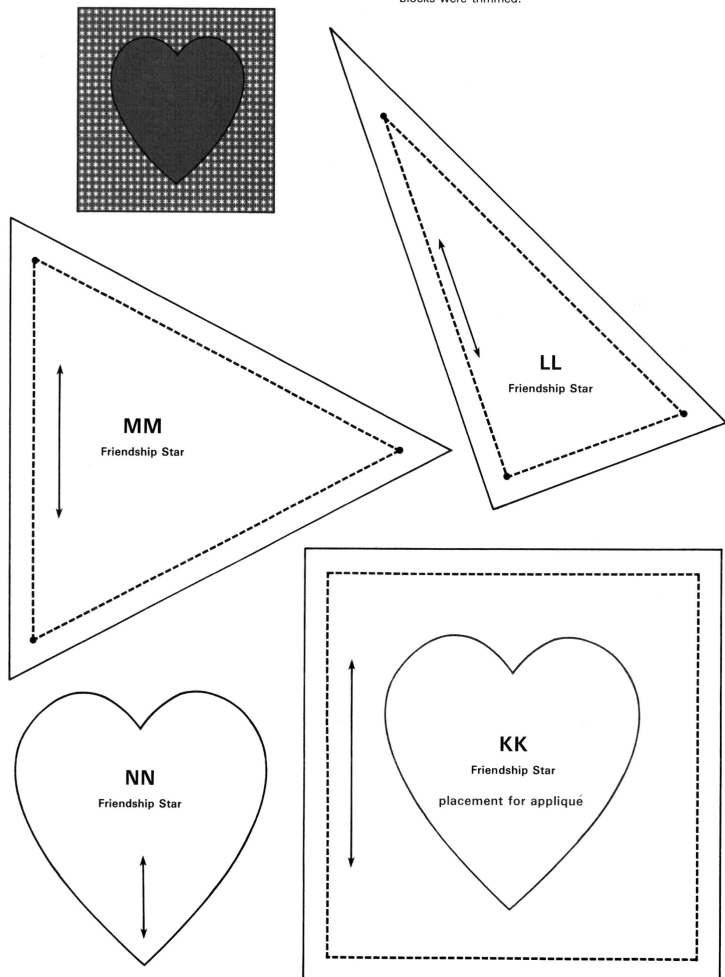

MM

Friendship Star

LL

Friendship Star

NN

Friendship Star

KK

Friendship Star

placement for appliqué

47

Lesson Nineteen

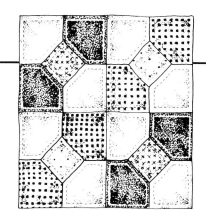

In this lesson you will make the **Bow Tie** block and learn about sewing into corners or setting in seams.

Fabric Key

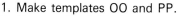

▦ background fabric	▦ medium fabric #1	▦ dark fabric #1
▦ light fabric	▦ medium fabric #2	

1. Make templates OO and PP.
2. Cut out the following:
   OO — eight from background fabric
   OO — four from medium fabric #1
   OO — four from dark fabric #1
   PP — two from light fabric
   PP — two from medium fabric #2
3. Sew one background fabric OO to one medium fabric #2 PP *(Fig. 19a)*. *(**Note:** If machine piecing, sew only between the dots when joining these pieces; the seam allowances must be left free in order to set in seams. If hand piecing, continue following drawn sewing line as usual.)* Sew one background fabric OO to same PP to make Unit 1 *(Fig. 19b)*. Repeat to make a total of two Unit 1's.

Fig. 19a   **Fig. 19b**

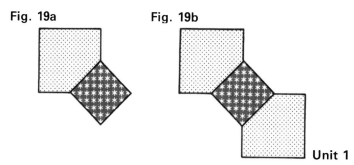

Unit 1

4. Sew one background fabric OO to one light fabric PP *(Fig. 19c)*. Sew one background fabric OO to same PP to make Unit 2 *(Fig. 19d)*. Repeat to make a total of two Unit 2's.

Fig. 19c   **Fig. 19d**

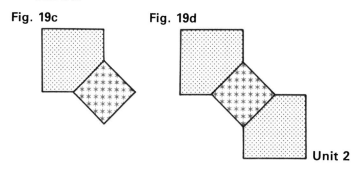

Unit 2

5. Follow **Sewing Into A Corner** to sew one dark fabric #1 OO to one Unit 1 *(Fig. 19e)*. Sew one dark fabric #1 OO to same Unit 1 to make Unit 3 *(Fig. 19f)*. Repeat to make a total of two Unit 3's.

Fig. 19e   **Fig. 19f**

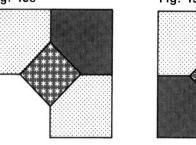
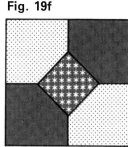

Unit 3

SEWING INTO A CORNER

When piecing blocks such as Bow Tie, LeMoyne Star, and Goose Tracks, there are times when the piece you add will have two or more adjoining edges to sew to the pieces you have already sewn. This is called sewing into a corner or setting in seams. To do so, you will sew the seam on one edge of the added piece; then, pivot the piece and sew the next seam.

Matching right sides, pin the new piece to the piece on the left. Stitch seam from the outer edge to the dot at the inside corner *(Fig. 19g)*.

Fig. 19g

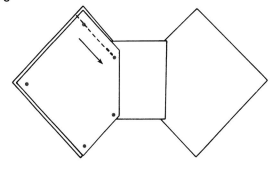

Pivot the added piece in order to sew the second seam. Pin and sew as before, beginning with the needle in the hole of the last stitch taken and ending at the second dot *(Fig. 19h)*.

Fig. 19h

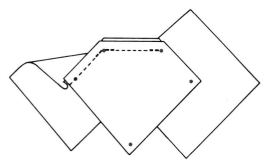

Pivot the added piece again and sew as before, beginning with the needle in the hole of the last stitch taken *(Fig. 19i)*.

Fig. 19i

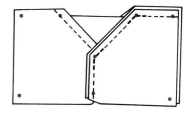

6. Sew one medium fabric #1 OO to one Unit 2 *(Fig. 19j)*. Sew one medium fabric #1 OO to same Unit 2 to make Unit 4 *(Fig. 19k)*. Repeat to make a total of two Unit 4's.

Fig. 19j   **Fig. 19k**

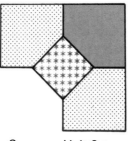
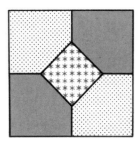

Unit 4

7. Sew one Unit 3 to one Unit 4 to make Row 1 *(Fig. 19l)*. Sew one Unit 3 to one Unit 4 to make Row 2.

Fig. 19l

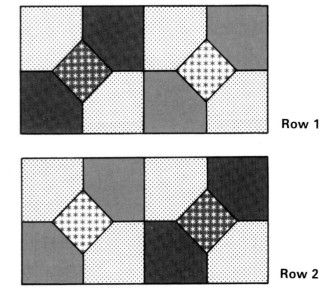

Row 1

Row 2

8. Sew Rows 1 and 2 together to complete Bow Tie block *(Fig. 19m)*.

Fig. 19m

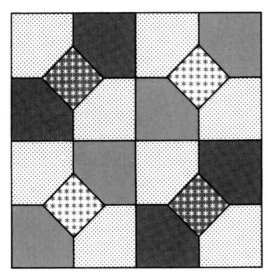

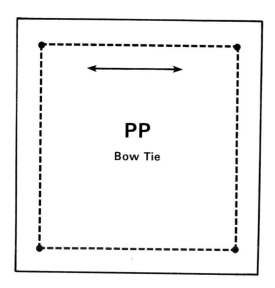

PP
Bow Tie

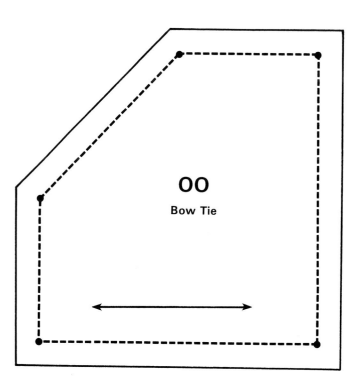

OO
Bow Tie

Lesson Twenty

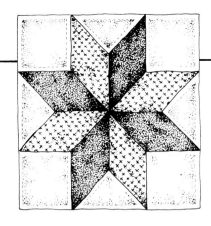

In this lesson you will make the **LeMoyne Star** block and review sewing into corners.

Fabric Key

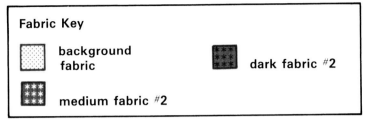

- background fabric
- medium fabric #2
- dark fabric #2

1. Make templates QQ and RR. You will also need template V (made previously).
2. Cut out the following:
   - V — four from background fabric
   - QQ — four from medium fabric #2
   - QQ — four from dark fabric #2
   - RR — four from background fabric
3. Sew one dark fabric #2 QQ to one medium fabric #2 QQ **(Fig. 20a)**. **(Note:** *If machine piecing, sew only between the dots when joining these pieces; the seam allowances must be left free in order to set in seams. If hand piecing, continue following drawn sewing line as usual.)* Sew one dark fabric #2 QQ to same medium fabric #2 QQ **(Fig. 20b)**. Sew one medium fabric #2 QQ to dark fabric #2 QQ to make Unit 1 **(Fig. 20c)**. Repeat to make Unit 2.

Fig. 20a   **Fig. 20b**

Fig. 20c

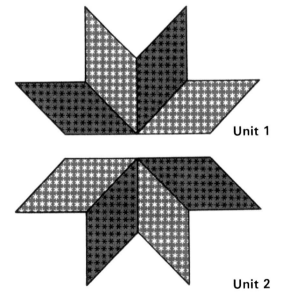

Unit 1

Unit 2

4. Sew Unit 1 and Unit 2 together to make Unit 3 **(Fig. 20d)**.

Fig. 20d

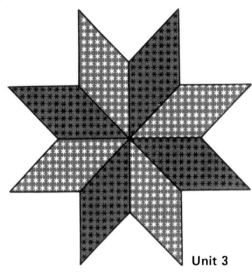

Unit 3

5. To reduce bulk in the center of the star, use your finger to open up and fan out seam allowances **(Fig. 20e)**.

Fig. 20e

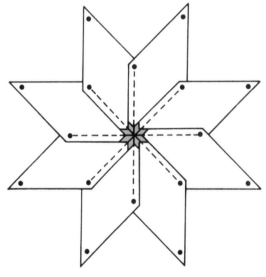

6. Follow **More Sewing Into Corners** to sew one V to Unit 3 *(Fig. 20f)*.

Fig. 20f

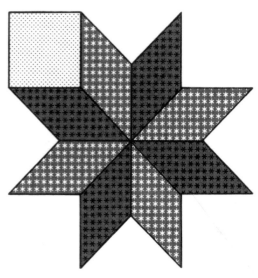

MORE SEWING INTO CORNERS

Matching right sides, pin the new piece to the piece on the left. Stitch seam from the dot at the outer edge to the dot at the inside corner *(Fig. 20g)*.

Fig. 20g

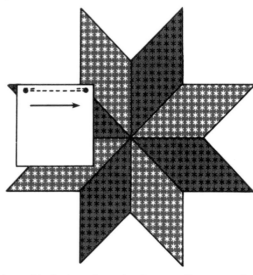

Pivot the added piece in order to sew the second seam. Pin and sew as before, beginning with the needle in the hole of the last stitch taken *(Fig. 20h)*.

Fig. 20h

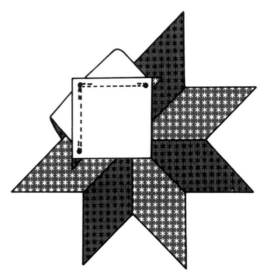

7. Sew remaining V's to Unit 3 *(Fig. 20i)*.

Fig. 20i

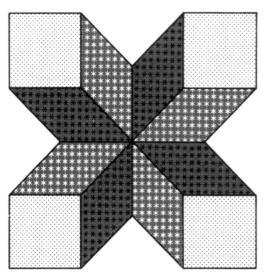

8. Sew one RR to Unit 3 *(Fig. 20j)*. Sew remaining RR's to Unit 3 to complete LeMoyne Star block *(Fig. 20k)*.

Fig. 20j

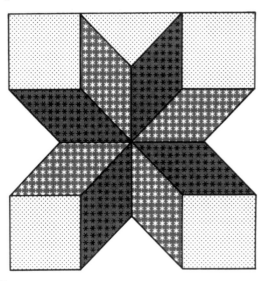

Fig. 20k

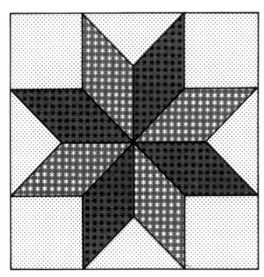

51

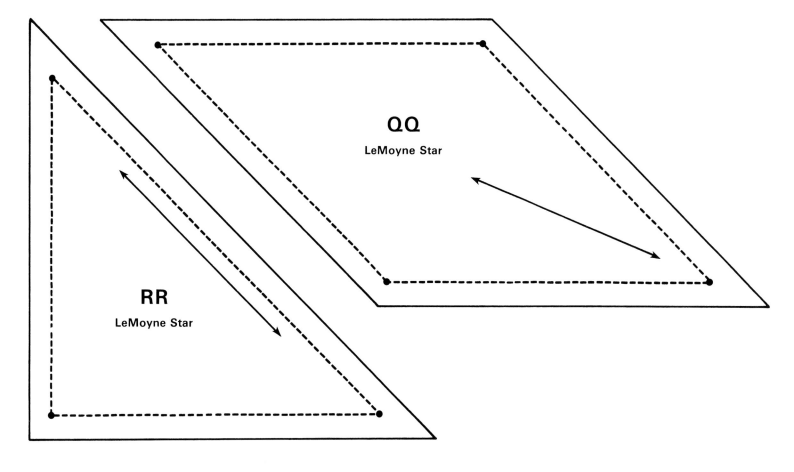

QQ

LeMoyne Star

RR

LeMoyne Star

Lesson Twenty-one

In this lesson you will make the **Goose Tracks** block and reinforce skills you have already learned.

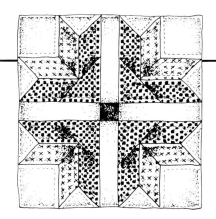

Fabric Key

▦	background fabric	▦	medium fabric #2
▦	medium fabric #1	▦	dark fabric #1

1. Make templates SS, TT, UU, VV, WW, and XX.
2. Cut out the following:

   SS — four from background fabric

   TT — four from medium fabric #1; four in reverse from medium fabric #1

   TT — four from medium fabric #2; four in reverse from medium fabric #2

   UU — four from medium fabric #1

   VV — eight from background fabric

   WW — four from background fabric

   XX — one from dark fabric #1

3. Sew one medium fabric #1 TT to one medium fabric #2 reverse TT to make Unit 1 *(Fig. 21a)*. **(Note:** *If machine piecing, sew only between the dots when joining these pieces; the seam allowances must be left free in order to set in seams. If hand piecing, continue following drawn sewing line as usual.)* Repeat to make a total of four Unit 1's.

Fig. 21a

Unit 1

4. Sew one medium fabric #2 TT to one medium fabric #1 reverse TT to make Unit 2 *(Fig. 21b)*. Repeat to make a total of four Unit 2's.

Fig. 21b

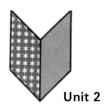

Unit 2

5. Sew one Unit 1 to one Unit 2 to make Unit 3 *(Fig. 21c)*. Repeat to make a total of four Unit 3's.

Fig. 21c

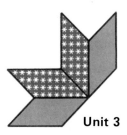

Unit 3

6. Sew one UU to one Unit 3 *(Fig. 21d)*. Sew one SS to same Unit 3 to make Unit 4. Repeat to make a total of four Unit 4's *(Fig. 21e)*.

Fig. 21d   **Fig. 21e**

   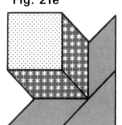

Unit 4

7. Sew one VV to one Unit 4. Sew one VV to same Unit 4 to make Unit 5 *(Fig. 21f)*. Repeat to make a total of four Unit 5's.

Fig. 21f

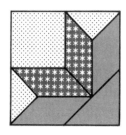

Unit 5

8. Sew one WW between two Unit 5's to make Row 1 *(Fig. 21g)*. Sew XX between two WW's to make Row 2. Sew one WW between two Unit 5's to make Row 3.

Fig. 21g

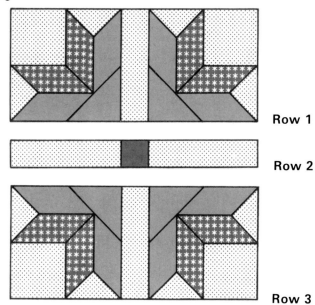

Row 1

Row 2

Row 3

9. Sew Rows 1, 2, and 3 together to complete Goose Tracks block *(Fig. 21h)*.

Fig. 21h

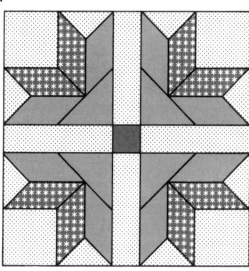

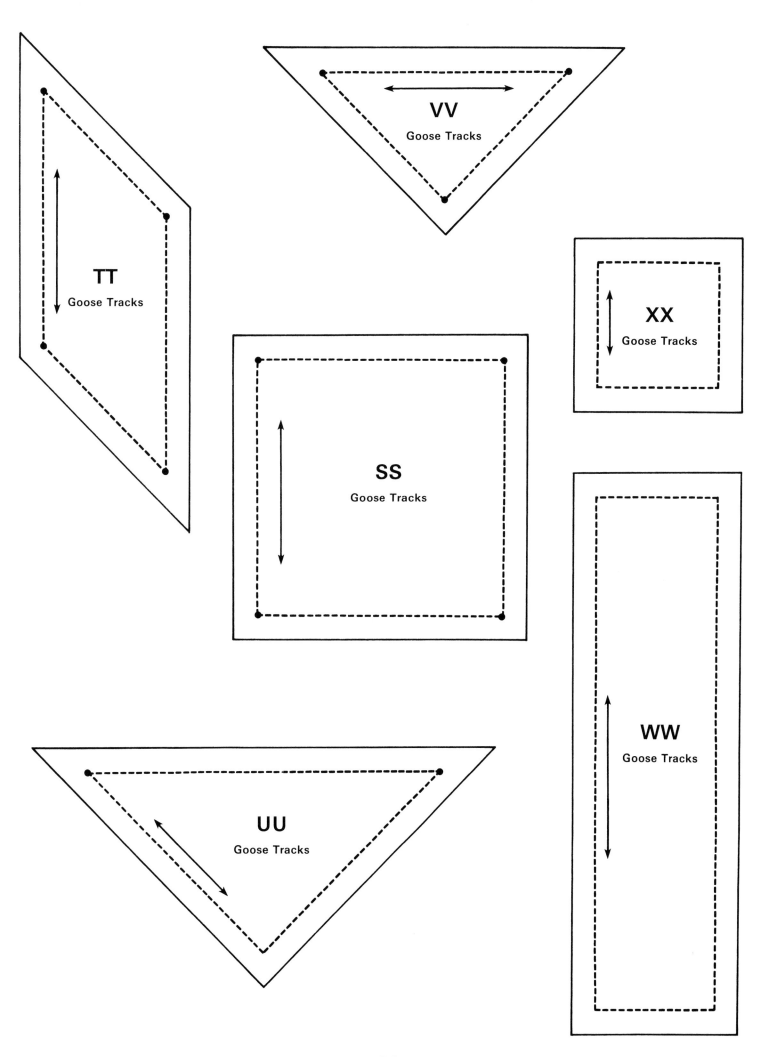

VV
Goose Tracks

TT
Goose Tracks

XX
Goose Tracks

SS
Goose Tracks

WW
Goose Tracks

UU
Goose Tracks

Lesson Twenty-two

In this lesson you will learn to add sashing and mitered borders to your quilt blocks. Sashing keeps the blocks in a sampler quilt from competing with each other and unifies the quilt. Borders frame the blocks and sashing. You will also learn about adding temporary strips of fabric to a quilt top to aid in quilting the borders.

ADDING SASHING

Seam allowances are included in sashing measurements. *(Note: If hand piecing, mark a ¼" seam allowance on each edge.)* When adding sashing strips to blocks, pin strip to block at ends; then, ease in any fullness while pinning remainder of edge. This makes the block fit the strip and should prevent wavy strips. When sewing, match right sides and raw edges and use a ¼" seam allowance. Press seam allowances toward sashing after adding each strip.

1. Cut fifteen 12½" strips from 100" strips.
2. Sew three strips between blocks indicated in **Fig. 22a** to make Row 1. Repeat to make Rows 2-5.

Fig. 22a

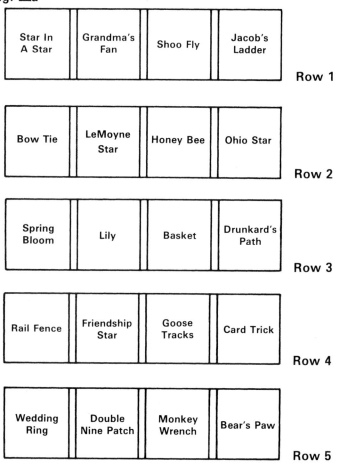

Star In A Star	Grandma's Fan	Shoo Fly	Jacob's Ladder	Row 1
Bow Tie	LeMoyne Star	Honey Bee	Ohio Star	Row 2
Spring Bloom	Lily	Basket	Drunkard's Path	Row 3
Rail Fence	Friendship Star	Goose Tracks	Card Trick	Row 4
Wedding Ring	Double Nine Patch	Monkey Wrench	Bear's Paw	Row 5

3. Matching short edges, fold one 56" strip in half; mark center of raw edges. Pin center of strip to center of bottom edge of Row 1. Pin ends of strip to ends of Row 1. Easing in any fullness, pin pieces together between ends. Sew strip in place *(Fig. 22b)*. Repeat for Rows 2-4.

Fig. 22b

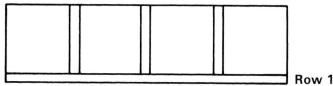

Row 1

4. Lay Row 1 on a flat surface. Place a ruler along seamline of sashing between blocks. Mark long sashing strip directly across from seamline. Repeat to mark sashing strip across from remaining seamlines *(Fig. 22c)*.

Fig. 22c

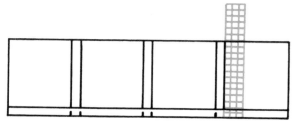

5. Match seamlines between blocks on Row 2 with marks on sashing strip *(Fig. 22d)*. Pin and sew pieces together, easing in any fullness between marks.

Fig. 22d

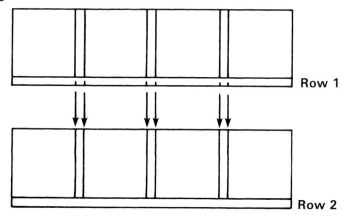

Row 1

Row 2

55

6. Repeat Steps 4-5 to add Rows 3-5 *(Fig. 22e)*.

Fig. 22e

ADDING MITERED BORDERS

Seam allowances are included in border measurements. *(**Note:** If hand piecing, mark a ¼" seam allowance on each edge.)* The border lengths include several extra inches for "insurance"; do not trim extra length until corners have been mitered. When sewing, match right sides and raw edges and use a ¼" seam allowance.

1. Sew one narrow 90" inner border strip to one wide 90" outer border strip; press seam allowances to one side. Repeat with remaining 90" border strips.
2. Sew one narrow 104" inner border strip to one wide 104" outer border strip; press seam allowances to one side. Repeat with remaining 104" border strips. *(**Note:** Strips combined in Steps 1 and 2 will be treated as one border strip for remainder of instructions. When attaching each combined border strip to quilt top, pin and sew long raw edge of **inner** border strip to edge of quilt top.)*
3. Matching short edges, fold one 90" border strip in half; mark center of raw edge. Pin center of border strip to top center of quilt top. From center of border strip, measure out 28" (which is ½ the width of the quilt top) in both directions and mark. Match marks on border strip with corners of quilt top and pin. Easing in any fullness, pin border strip to quilt top between center and corners.
4. Sew border strip to quilt top beginning and ending **exactly** ¼" from each corner of quilt top, backstitching at beginning and end of stitching line *(Fig. 22f)*. Do **not** sew into seam allowance.

Fig. 22f

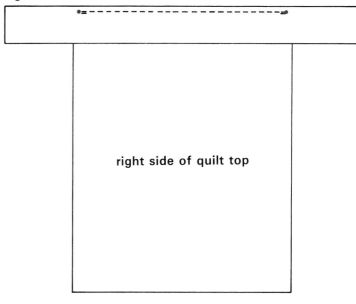

right side of quilt top

5. Repeat Steps 3 and 4 to sew remaining 90" border strip to bottom edge of quilt top.
6. To temporarily move top and bottom border strips out of the way, fold ends of strips and pin as shown in **Fig. 22g**.

Fig. 22g

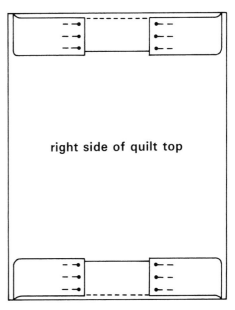

right side of quilt top

7. Matching short edges, fold one 104" border strip in half; mark center of raw edge. Pin center of border strip to center of quilt top at side. From center of border strip, measure out 35" (which is ½ the length of the quilt top) in both directions and mark. Match marks on border strip with corners of quilt top and pin. Easing in any fullness, pin border strip to quilt top between center and corners.

8. Sew border strip to quilt top beginning and ending **exactly** ¼" from each corner of quilt top, backstitching at beginning and end of stitching line *(Fig. 22h)*. *(Note: Stitching should begin and end exactly at ends of previous stitching lines.)* Do **not** sew into seam allowance.

Fig. 22h

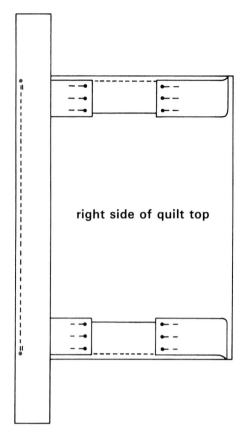

right side of quilt top

9. Repeat Steps 7 and 8 to add remaining 104" border strip to quilt top on opposite side. Press seam allowances toward border strips.
10. Lay quilt top right side down on a flat surface. Overlap top and bottom border strips over side border strips.
11. Mark bottom strip on outer edge at the point where strips overlap *(Fig. 22i)*.

Fig. 22i

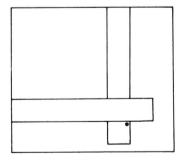

12. Matching right sides and raw edges, bring strips together with marked strip on top. Use ruler to draw a line from the mark on the outer edge of strip to the end of the stitching line *(Fig. 22j)*.

Fig. 22j

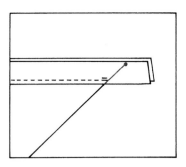

13. Pin strips together along drawn line, making sure seams of narrow and wide border strips match. Sew directly on drawn line, backstitching at beginning and end of stitching *(Fig. 22k)*.

Fig. 22k

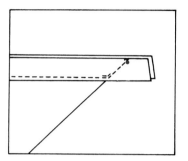

14. Turn mitered corner right side up. Check to see that there is not a gap at the inner end of the seam. Also check that border seams match and that corner does not pucker. If necessary, use seam ripper to remove seam; carefully pin and sew seam again.
15. Trim seam allowances to ¼" *(Fig. 22l)*. Press seam allowances to one side.

Fig. 22l

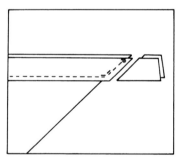

16. Repeat Steps 11-15 to miter each remaining corner.

ATTACHING TEMPORARY BORDERS
Quilting the borders of a quilt can be awkward or difficult because they cannot be held securely in a hoop. To aid in quilting the borders, you may wish to add temporary strips of fabric to the quilt top. These strips are not quilted. They are basted to the outer edges of the quilt top and are removed when quilting is complete.

Cut two 5" x 93" strips of fabric. *(Note: These strips may be pieced, if necessary.)* Using a ⅛" seam allowance, baste strips to sides of quilt top. Cut two 5" x 78½" strips of fabric. Baste strips to top and bottom of quilt top.

Lesson Twenty-Three

In this lesson, you will learn how to mark each type of quilting line, how to prepare your quilt layers for quilting, and how to use the Quilting Stitch.

The quilting diagrams included in this section show all quilting lines for each block. Familiarize yourself with **Types of Quilting**, below, to learn which quilting lines need to be marked and which ones do not. After marking the necessary quilting lines on each block and the quilting lines on the outer border, you will prepare the backing and baste the quilt layers together. Then, use the quilting diagrams as a reference when quilting each block.

TYPES OF QUILTING

(Note: The diagram for the Grandma's Fan block shows examples of each type of quilting and how they are indicated on all diagrams.)

In The Ditch — Quilting close to the edge of a seam or appliqué. This type of quilting does not need to be marked, but is indicated on diagrams by dashed lines running very close to solid lines. When quilting In The Ditch, quilt on the side **opposite** the seam allowance.

Outline — Quilting approximately ¼" from a seam or appliqué. Indicated on diagrams by dashed lines a short distance from solid lines. This type of quilting may be marked to ensure an accurate quilting line. It is easiest to mark these lines before basting quilt layers together. Use a ruler to mark straight lines. Or, place ¼"w masking tape on the quilt to mark straight lines; then, quilt directly beside the edge of the tape. *(Note: Do not leave the tape on the quilt any longer than is necessary. Remove the tape when you are through quilting a line, and any time you put the quilt away. The tape may damage the fabric if left on for a long period of time.)* To mark curved lines, carefully mark ¼" from seam or appliqué, checking at frequent intervals with a ruler. After a short amount of quilting experience, Outline quilting will feel more natural to you and marking these lines may not be necessary.

Ornamental — Quilting decorative lines or designs. Indicated on diagrams by dashed lines. This type of quilting should also be marked before you baste quilt layers together. Patterns for most Ornamental quilting designs are on pgs. 65-67. To mark these lines, you can trace the pattern onto the fabric and not have to make a template. If necessary, use a light table or sunny window to see patterns through darker fabrics. Quilting lines on outer border are marked using a template.

MARKING QUILTING LINES

Instructions for marking each block are included with the diagrams. Diagrams also indicate where each block will be quilted In The Ditch.

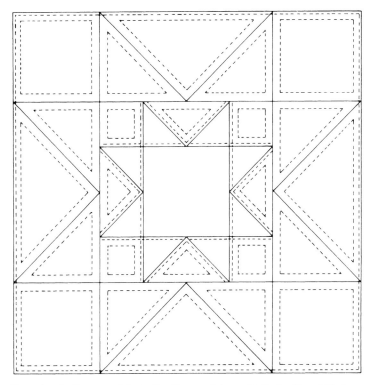

Star In A Star — Mark Outline quilting. Quilt In The Ditch as shown. Quilt along drawn lines.

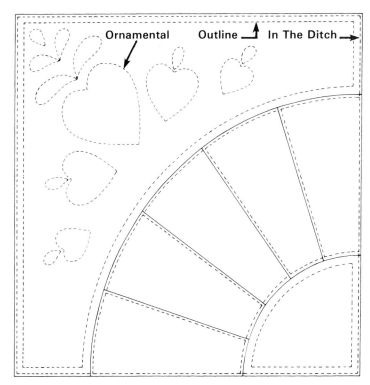

Grandma's Fan — Mark Outline quilting. If you did not make template AA from clear plastic, make a quilting template from typing paper. To do so, trace quilting lines, dashed line, and fold line of pattern (pgs. 37-38) onto typing paper. Turn typing paper over and trace design onto back of paper.
Matching outer edges, place fabric right side up over template and trace quilting design onto half of fabric. Turn template over and trace design onto remaining half of fabric. Quilt In The Ditch as shown. Quilt along drawn lines.

Shoo Fly — Mark Outline quilting. Center one background fabric square over quilting pattern (pg. 65) and trace design onto fabric. Repeat for each background fabric square. Quilt In The Ditch as shown. Quilt along drawn lines.

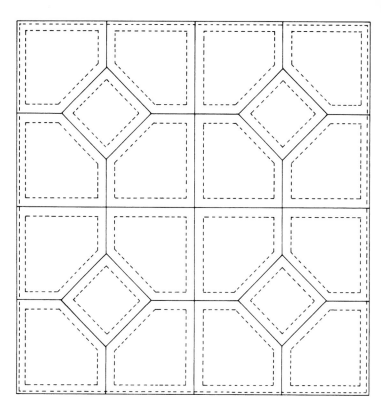

Bow Tie — Mark Outline quilting. Quilt In The Ditch as shown. Quilt along drawn lines.

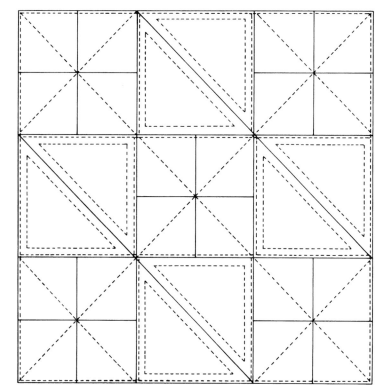

Jacob's Ladder — Mark Outline and Ornamental quilting. Quilt In The Ditch as shown. Quilt along drawn lines.

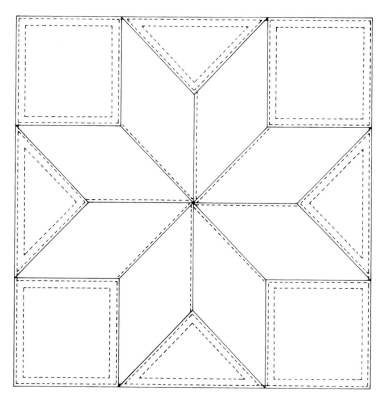

LeMoyne Star — Mark Outline quilting. Quilt In The Ditch as shown. Quilt along drawn lines.

Honey Bee — Mark Outline quilting. Quilt In The Ditch as shown. Quilt along drawn lines.

Spring Bloom — Mark Outline quilting. Place one corner of fabric over quilting pattern (pg. 66) and trace bow onto fabric. Repeat for each remaining corner. Quilt In The Ditch as shown. Quilt along drawn lines.

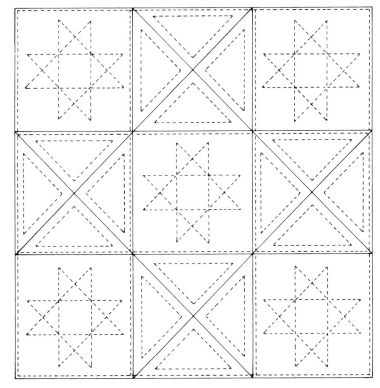

Ohio Star — Mark Outline quilting. Place center square over quilting pattern (pg. 65) and trace design onto fabric. Repeat for each background square. Quilt In The Ditch as shown. Quilt along drawn lines.

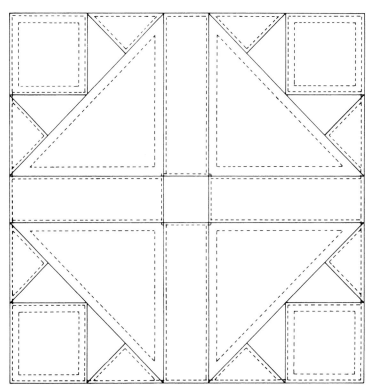

Lily — Mark Outline quilting. Quilt In The Ditch as shown. Quilt along drawn lines.

Basket — Mark Outline quilting and Ornamental quilting on basket. Place fabric over quilting pattern (pg. 67) and trace design onto fabric. Quilt In The Ditch as shown. Quilt along drawn lines.

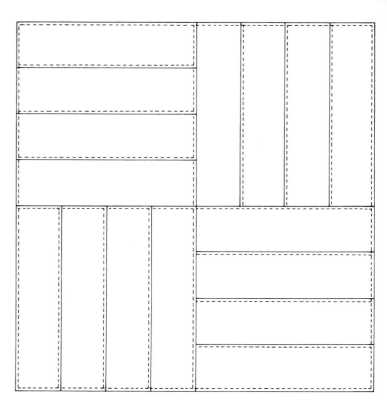

Rail Fence — Quilt In The Ditch as shown.

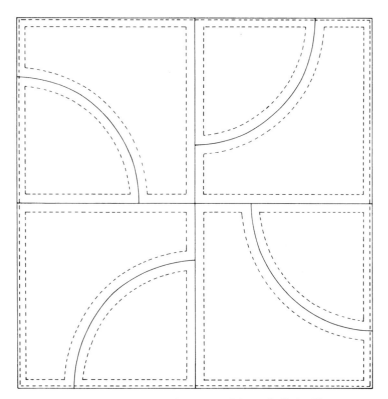

Drunkard's Path — Mark Outline quilting. Quilt In The Ditch as shown. Quilt along drawn lines.

Friendship Star — Mark Outline quilting. Place one background fabric square over quilting pattern (pg. 66) and trace heart onto fabric. Repeat for each corner square. Quilt In The Ditch as shown. Quilt along drawn lines.

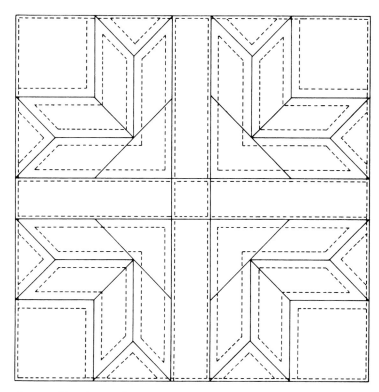

Goose Tracks — Mark Outline quilting. Quilt In The Ditch as shown. Quilt along drawn lines.

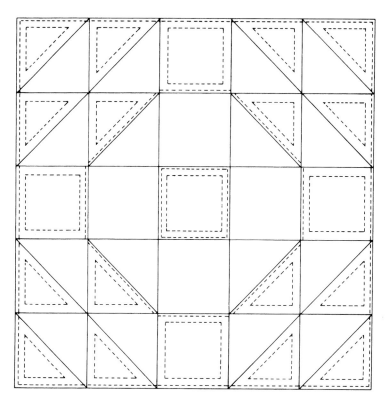

Wedding Ring — Mark Outline quilting. Quilt In The Ditch as shown. Quilt along drawn lines.

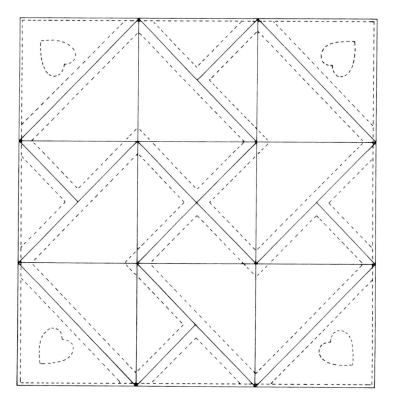

Card Trick — Mark Outline quilting. Place one corner of block over quilting pattern (pg. 67) and trace design onto fabric. Repeat for each remaining corner. Quilt In The Ditch as shown. Quilt along drawn lines.

Double Nine Patch — Place one background fabric square over quilting pattern (pg. 67) and trace design onto fabric. Repeat for each remaining background fabric square. Quilt In The Ditch as shown. Quilt along drawn lines.

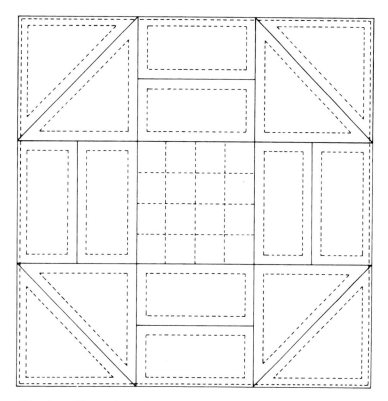

Monkey Wrench — Mark Outline quilting. For Ornamental quilting on center square, draw a grid of lines 1" apart. Quilt In The Ditch as shown. Quilt along drawn lines.

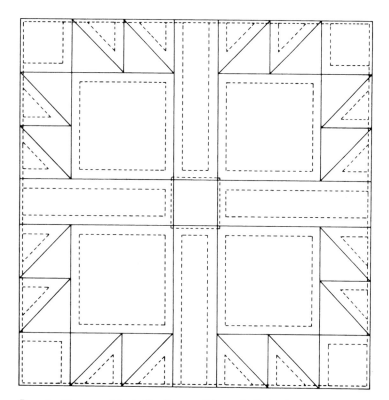

Bear's Paw — Mark Outline quilting. Quilt In The Ditch as shown. Quilt along drawn lines.

Sashing — Quilt In The Ditch along each seamline where sashing and inner border meet.

Inner border — Quilt In The Ditch along seamline of inner and outer border.

Outer border — Follow Steps 1-9 to mark diagonal quilting lines.

1. To make template for outer border, draw and cut out a 12" square from lightweight cardboard or clear plastic. Use ruler to draw a line diagonally across square *(Fig. 23a)*.

Fig. 23a

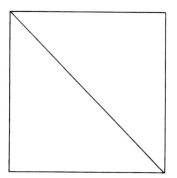

2. Draw a second line parallel to first and 1½" from first line *(Fig. 23b)*.

Fig. 23b

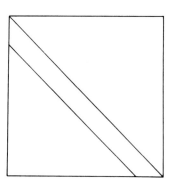

3. Draw a third line 1½" from bottom of square and from second line to edge of square *(Fig. 23c)*. Cut out template and mark edges A, B, and C as shown in **Fig. 23d**.

Fig. 23c   **Fig. 23d**

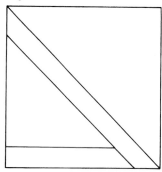   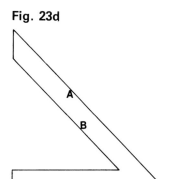

63

4. To mark quilting lines on outer border, lightly mark center on each edge of quilt from seamline of outer border to edge. Place template on bottom strip of outer border so that edge C lines up with bottom edge of border and edge A meets top of center mark *(Fig. 23e)*.

Fig. 23e

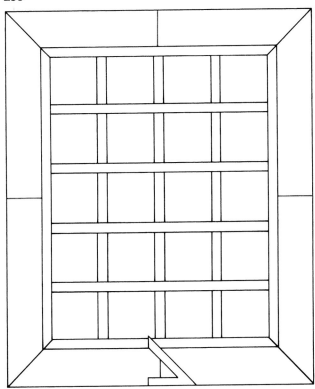

5. Use marking tool to draw on quilt top along edge A. Top of drawn line should meet center mark. Move template over, lining up edge B with previous drawn line. Draw along edge A. Repeat to draw five or six lines toward corner.
6. Move template to corner of quilt, lining up edge A with mitered seam *(Fig. 23f)*.

Fig. 23f

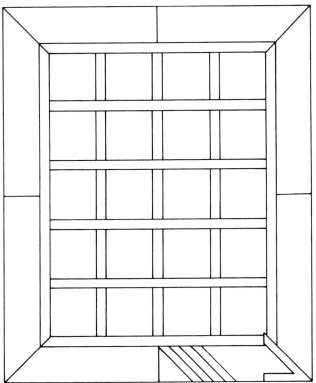

7. Draw along edge B. Move template over, lining up edge A with previous drawn line; finish drawing line to bottom edge of border. Repeat to draw five or six lines toward center. If the template does not fit an exact number of times on border, make slight adjustments in spaces between lines. Turn the template over and mark quilting lines slanting in the opposite direction.
8. To mark shorter lines at center, place template on quilt, lining up edge A with drawn line closest to center. Mark along edge B from center line to edge of quilt. Repeat to mark remaining short lines *(Fig. 23g)*.

Fig. 23g

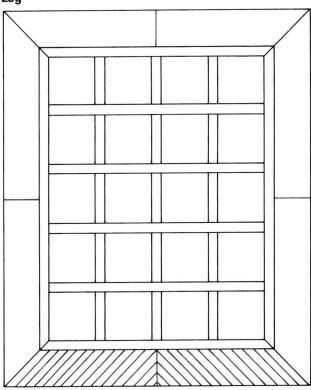

9. Repeat Steps 4-8 to mark quilting lines on remaining outer border strips.
10. Quilt along drawn lines. Quilt In The Ditch along mitered seam at each corner.

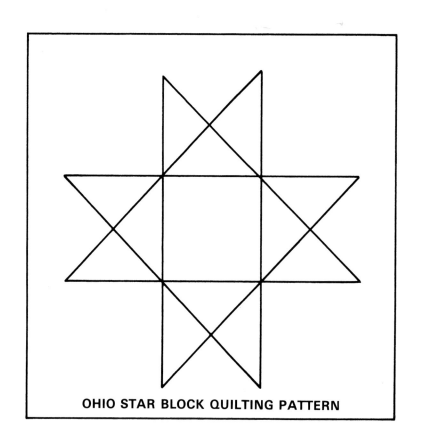

OHIO STAR BLOCK QUILTING PATTERN

SHOO FLY BLOCK QUILTING PATTERN

FRIENDSHIP STAR BLOCK QUILTING PATTERN

SPRING BLOOM BLOCK QUILTING PATTERN

CARD TRICK BLOCK QUILTING PATTERN

BASKET BLOCK QUILTING PATTERN

DOUBLE NINE PATCH QUILTING PATTERN

PREPARING BACKING AND BATTING

The backing and batting should be a few inches larger on all sides than the quilt top to allow for the quilt top shifting slightly during quilting. Some fabrics, such as muslin, are available in a 90" width. Using a 90" wide fabric will eliminate the need to piece the backing.

If you use a fabric that is not available in a 90" width, you will need to piece the backing. The backing should be pieced with the seams away from the center. This reduces the stress in the areas of the quilt that are folded most often.

To piece backing using 44/45"w fabric, cut fabric into two lengths of three yards each. Matching right sides and long edges, pin fabric pieces together. Using a ½" seam allowance, sew pieces together along both long edges *(Fig. 23h)*.

Match seams (as when ironing pants) and press along one fold *(Fig. 23i)*.

Fig. 23h   **Fig. 23i**

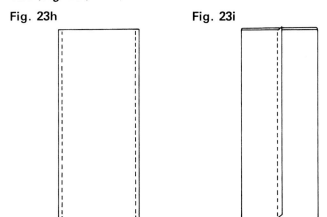

Cut along pressed fold, unfold fabric, and press seam allowances open *(Fig. 23j)*.

Fig. 23j

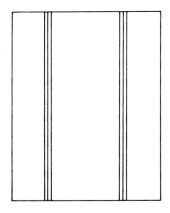

Cut batting same size as backing.

ASSEMBLING THE QUILT

Examine wrong side of quilt top closely and trim any seam allowances or clip any threads that may show through to the front of the quilt. Check quilting lines to make sure that all necessary lines have been marked. Press quilt top if necessary.

Place backing fabric **wrong** side up on a flat surface. Place batting on wrong side of backing fabric. Smooth out batting, being sure to handle batting gently so as not to tear it. Center quilt top **right** side up on batting. Pin all layers together, placing pins approximately 4" apart and smoothing out bulges or wrinkles. Beginning each line of basting in the center and working toward the edges, use very long stitches to baste all layers together as shown in **Fig. 23k**. *(Note: A spoon is very helpful for catching the tip of the needle on the quilt top when basting.)* Basting lines should be about 3-4" apart, with outer basting lines ½" from edges of quilt top. It is not necessary to baste temporary borders. Remove pins.

Fig. 23k

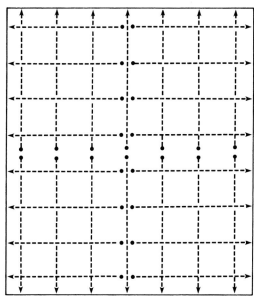

QUILTING

Secure center of quilt in hoop. Check quilt top and backing to make sure they are smooth.

The **Quilting Stitch** is a basic Running Stitch that forms a broken line on quilt top and backing. Stitches on quilt top and backing should be equal in length. Thread quilting needle with an 18-20" length of quilting thread; a longer length may tangle or fray. Do not double thread; make a small knot in one end. Beginning in the center of the quilt, insert needle into quilt top and batting approximately ½" from where you wish to begin quilting. Bring needle up at the point where you wish to begin *(Fig. 23l)*; when knot catches on quilt top, give thread a quick, short pull to pop knot through fabric into batting *(Fig. 23m)*.

Fig. 23l

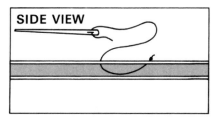

Fig. 23m

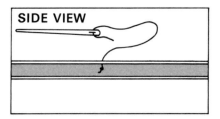

Holding the needle with your sewing hand and placing your other hand underneath the fabric, take the tip of the needle down through all layers. *(Note: Right-handers work from top to bottom or right to left. Left-handers work from top to bottom or left to right.)* As soon as the needle touches your underneath finger, use that finger to push only the tip of the needle back up through layers. *(Note: The amount of the needle showing above the fabric determines the length of the quilting stitch. We recommend that beginners take 5-7 stitches per inch.)* Rocking the needle up and down, take 3-6 stitches before bringing the needle and thread completely through the layers *(Fig. 23n)*. Check the back of the quilt to make sure stitches are going through all layers. If you are quilting through a seam allowance or quilting a curve or corner, you may need to take one stitch at a time.

Fig. 23n

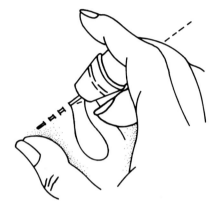

When you reach the end of your thread, tie a small knot close to fabric and pop knot into batting; clip thread close to fabric. As in hand piecing, try to keep stitches straight and even. With practice, stitches will also be small.

It is very important to quilt from the center of the quilt out. If you try to quilt one side of the quilt and then the other, or quilt one block and then skip over to another block, you will find it hard to keep the quilt from puckering. Stop and move your hoop as often as necessary. You do not have to tie a knot every time you move your hoop; you may leave the thread dangling and pick it back up when you reach that part of the quilt again.

When you have finished quilting, remove all basting stitches **except** those that are ½" from edges of quilt top; these will secure the edges of the quilt while the binding is being attached. Remove temporary borders. Trim batting and backing even with quilt top.

Lesson Twenty-four

In this lesson you will learn how to make a continuous bias binding and attach doubled binding with mitered corners. Making and attaching binding in this manner will protect the edges of your quilt especially well and make it last longer. Binding with a bias edge will wear longer than binding cut on the straight grain. Doubled binding provides a double thickness of fabric to cover the raw edges of the quilt.

MAKING CONTINUOUS BIAS STRIP BINDING
Binding may be purchased at the store, but making your own binding allows you to coordinate your binding color with the colors in your quilt.

1. Cut a 36" square from binding fabric. Fold square in half diagonally; cut on fold to make two triangles.
2. With right sides together and using a ¼" seam allowance, sew triangles together *(Fig. 24a)*; press seam allowances open.

Fig. 24a

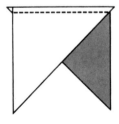

3. On wrong side of fabric, draw lines 2" apart, parallel to long edges *(Fig. 24b)*. Cut off any remaining fabric less than 2".

Fig. 24b

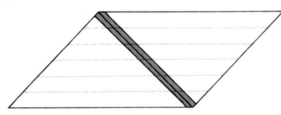

4. Mark seamlines ¼" from short edges of fabric *(Fig. 24c)*.

Fig. 24c

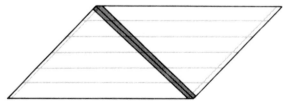

5. With right sides inside, bring short edges together to form a tube *(Fig. 24d)*.

Fig. 24d

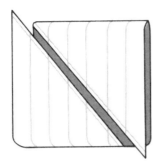

6. Match raw edges so that first line of top section meets second line of bottom section. Insert pins through drawn lines at the point where the drawn lines intersect and make sure the pins go through intersections on both sides *(Fig. 24e)*. Carefully pin edges together. Sew edges together along drawn seamlines.

Fig. 24e

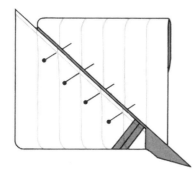

7. To cut continuous strip, begin cutting along first drawn line *(Fig. 24f)*. Continue cutting along drawn line around tube.

Fig. 24f

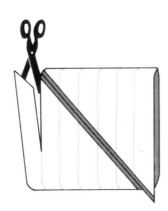

8. Trim each end of bias strip as shown in **Fig. 24g**.

Fig. 24g

9. Matching wrong sides and long edges, fold strip in half; press *(Fig. 24h)*. Wrap binding around a piece of cardboard until ready to use.

Fig. 24h

ATTACHING BINDING WITH MITERED CORNERS

1. Fold one end of binding diagonally; press *(Fig. 24i)*.

Fig. 24i

2. Matching raw edges and beginning with pressed end approximately 20" from a corner, pin binding to front of quilt along one side. Lay binding around quilt to make sure that seams in binding will not end up at a corner. Adjust binding if necessary.
3. When you reach the first corner, use your marking tool to mark ¼" from corner of quilt top *(Fig. 24j)*.

Fig. 24j

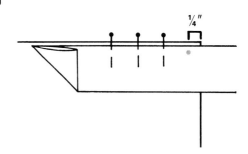

4. Using a ¼" seam allowance, sew binding to quilt top, backstitching at beginning of stitching and when you reach the mark *(Fig. 24k)*. Lift needle out of fabric and clip thread.

Fig. 24k

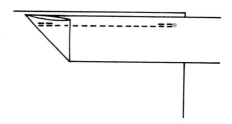

5. Fold binding as shown in **Figs. 24l** and **24m** and pin binding to adjacent side, matching raw edges.

Fig. 24l

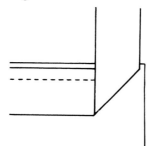

Fig. 24m

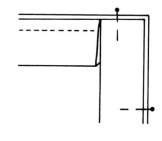

6. When you reach the next corner, use marking tool to mark ¼" from edge of quilt top.
7. Beginning at edge of quilt top, sew binding to quilt top *(Fig. 24n)*; backstitch when you reach the mark. Lift needle out of fabric and clip thread.

Fig. 24n

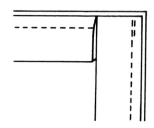

8. Repeat Steps 5-7 to continue stitching binding to quilt top. Leaving a 2" overlap, trim off excess binding. Stitch overlap in place.
9. On one edge of quilt, fold binding over to quilt backing and pin pressed edge in place, covering stitching line *(Fig. 24o)*. On adjacent side, fold binding over, forming a mitered corner *(Fig. 24p)*. Repeat to pin remainder of binding in place.

Fig. 24o   **Fig. 24p**

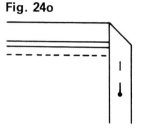   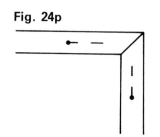

10. Whipstitch binding to backing.

Lesson Twenty-five

In this lesson, you will learn to sign and date your quilt.

Signing and dating your quilt is a very important step in quiltmaking. It will let future generations know who made the quilt and when it was made. You may wish to add other personal information. Was the quilt made in honor of a special occasion, such as a wedding or the birth of a baby? Was the quilt made as a gift? The personalizing is basically writing your information on a small piece of fabric and appliquéing it to the backing.

1. Cut a 10" square of fabric and a 9" square of freezer paper.
2. Center freezer paper shiny side down on wrong side of fabric. Iron freezer paper to fabric to stabilize fabric, holding iron on fabric for 3-5 seconds. *(**Note:** Do not leave iron on freezer paper any longer as it may make freezer paper difficult to remove from fabric.)*
3. If you wish to write your information inside a shape such as a heart or flower, make a template for the shape and draw around template on right side of fabric.
4. Use a permanent fine point marker to write the information inside the drawn line. If desired, add a drawn design.
5. Remove freezer paper from back of fabric and trim fabric to 3⁄16" outside drawn line.
6. Position shape on back of quilt and appliqué shape to quilt, being careful to stitch through backing only.

Index _____